DOODLEWORLDS

A whimsical and fun colouring book from
Angela Porter

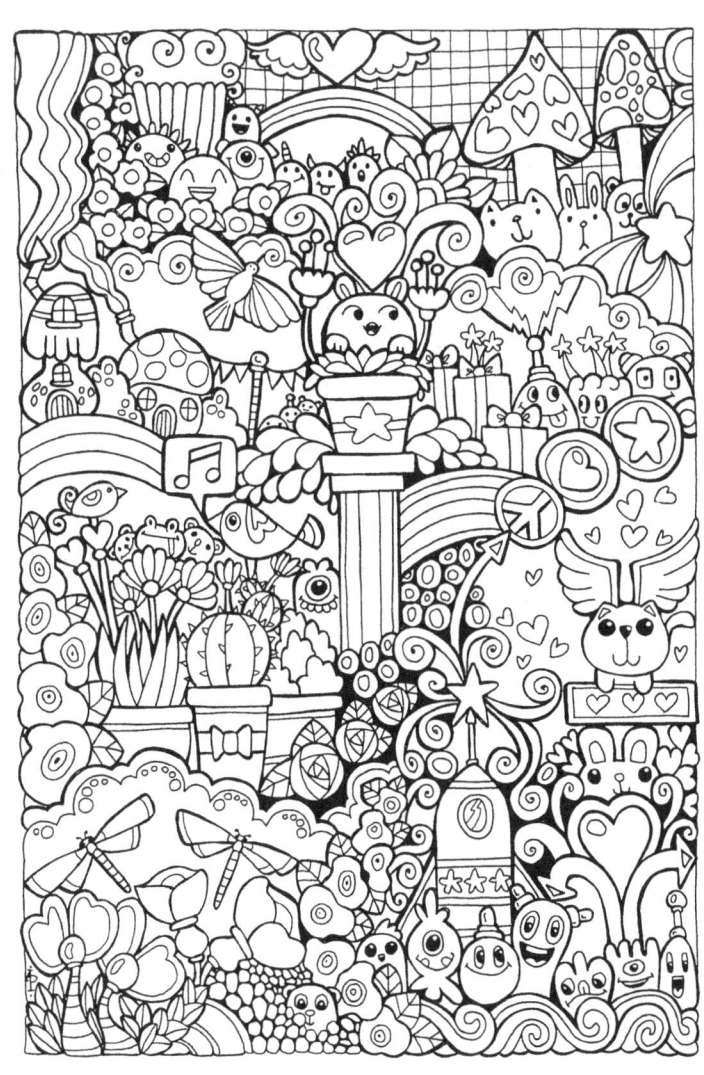

Take a whimsical journey through the imaginative Doodleworlds, where creatures and critters roam through seas and skies, woods and cities, encountering all kinds of items along the way. Use the magic of colour to bring their worlds alive.

Dedication

I would like to thank all who have believed in me and my art, helping me to develop my skills in previous books. My thanks go especially to **Jeannine Dillon**, **Diane Rubin** *and* **Jason Schneider**, *amongst others.*

My thanks also go to one dear friend who has supported me and believed in me even during my darkest times over nearly two decades now—thank you **Kevin**.

My thanks also go to all of you, my brave, bold and wonderful colorists who do such marvellous work in bringing my line art alive. To you I say, there's no colouring Police, no one to tell you that trees aren't purple and grass isn't pink, and that you really shouldn't go outside the lines. There are no rules, on the ones you set yourself. There's also no mistakes, only happy accidents and creative opportunities.

Last, but not least, my thanks go to **Brett** *and* **Krystal**, *who bravely set up and manage the* **'Angela Porter's Coloring Book Fans'** *group on facebook. Thank you for setting up a lovely community where people can share their work not just with each other but with me, so I can see the life you breathe into my line art with the skilful and joyful use of your pens and pencils.*

Thank you one and all.

Find me online:

Facebook : Angela Porter Illustrator

Instagram : Angela Porter Illustrator

Blog : Artwyrd.com

deviantART : Artwyrd.deviantART.com

Etsy: www.etsy.com/uk/shop/Artwyrd, where a pdf version of the book is available

Copyright

Copyright © 2017 by Angela Porter

All rights reserved.

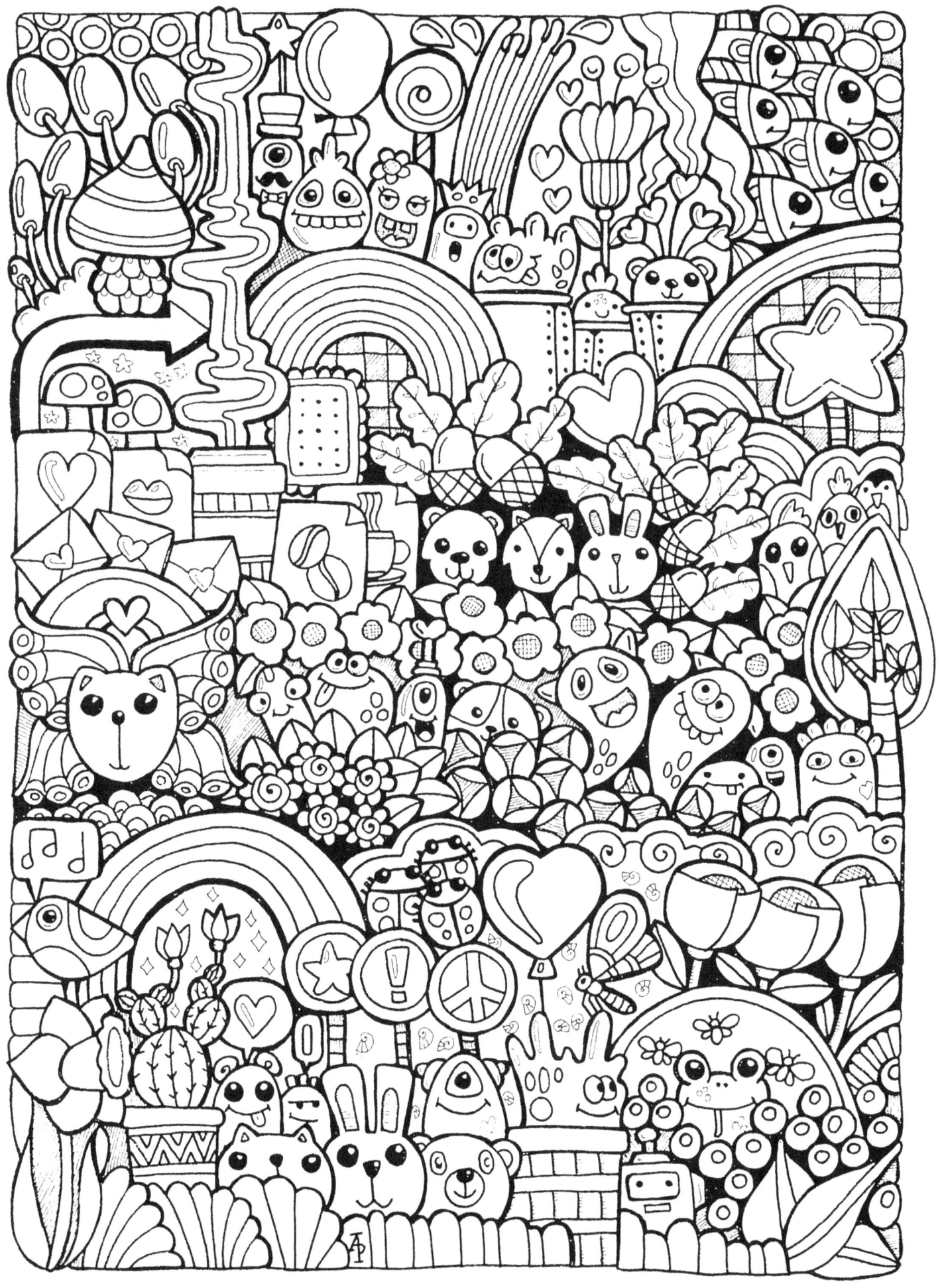

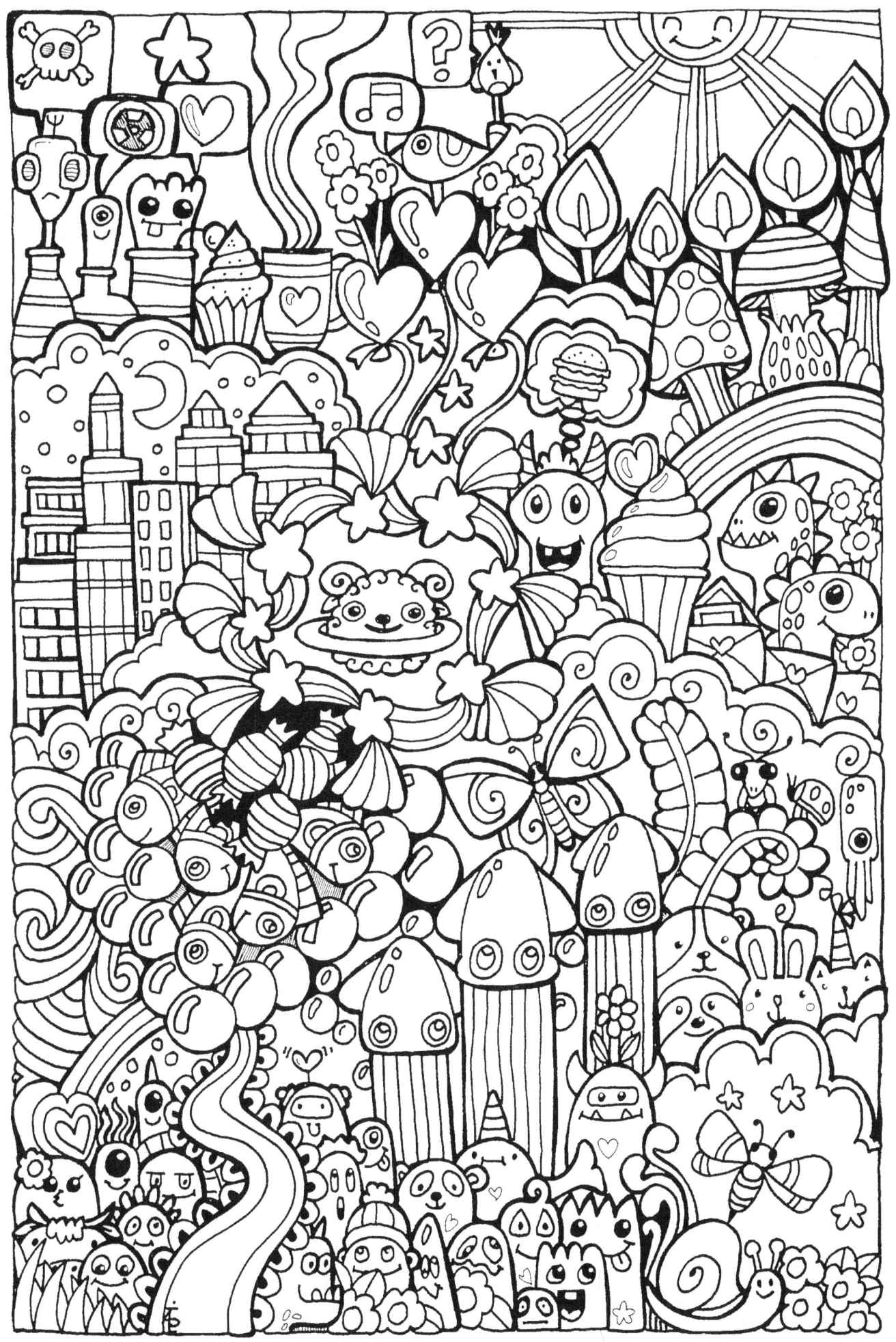

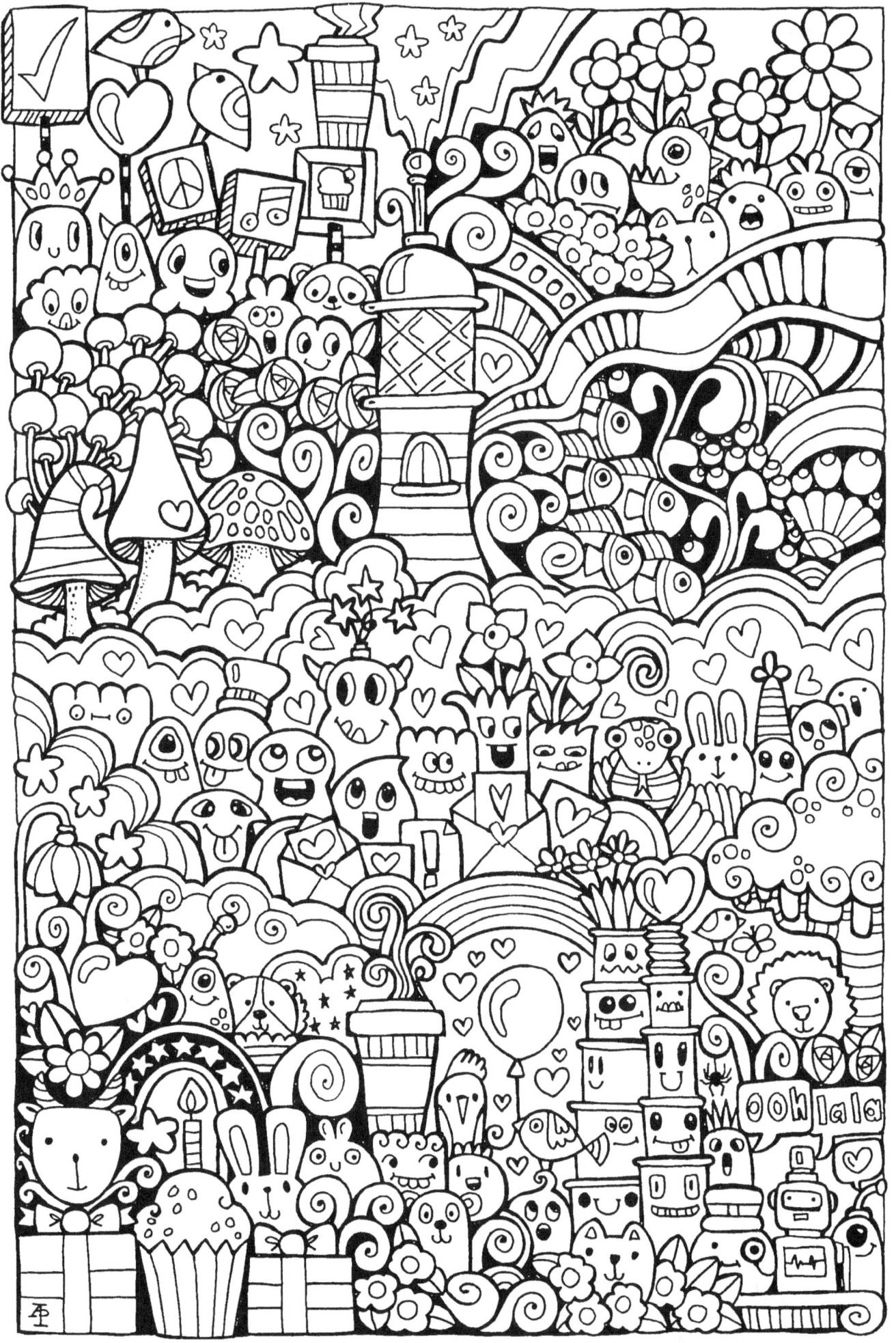

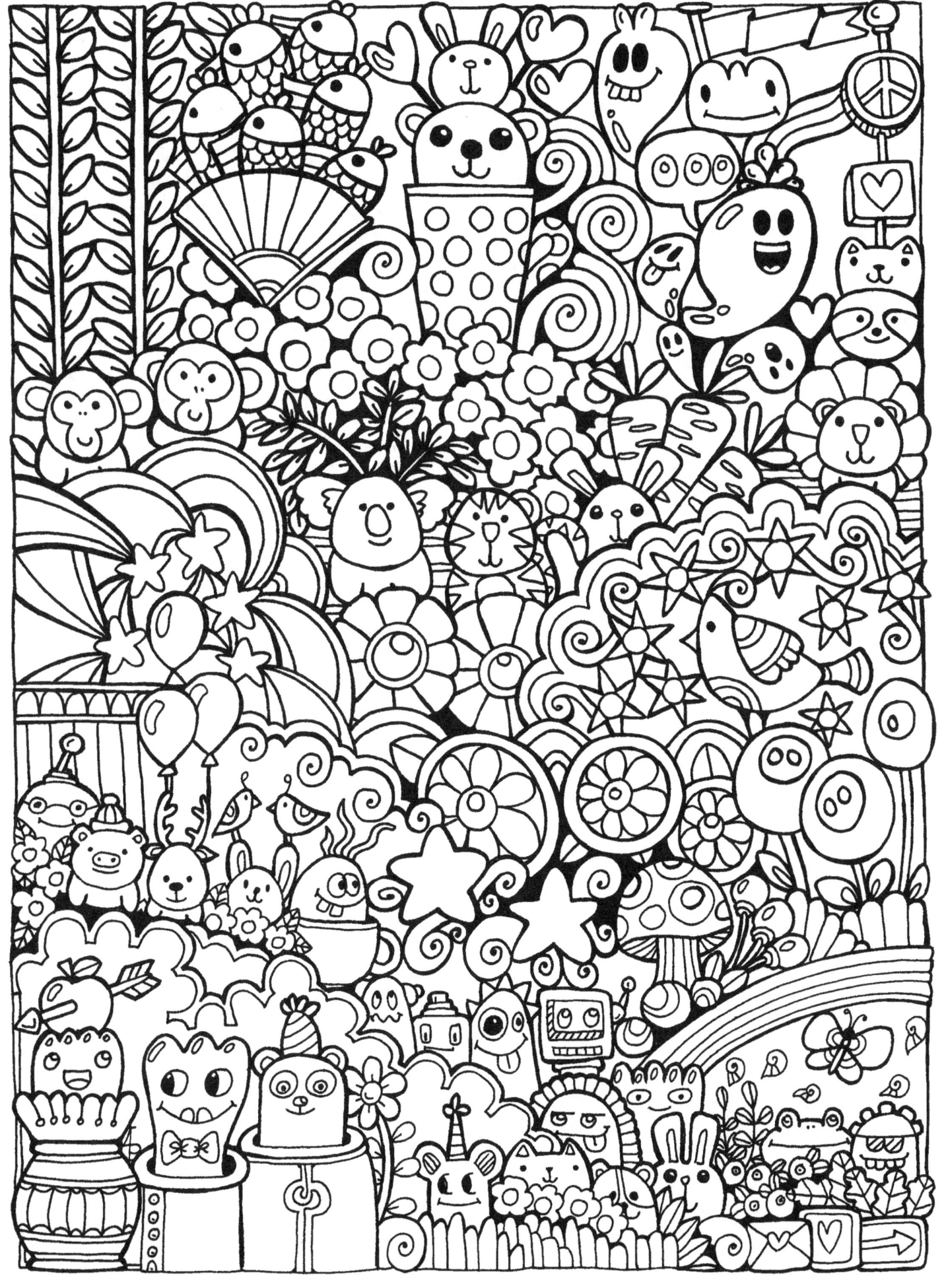

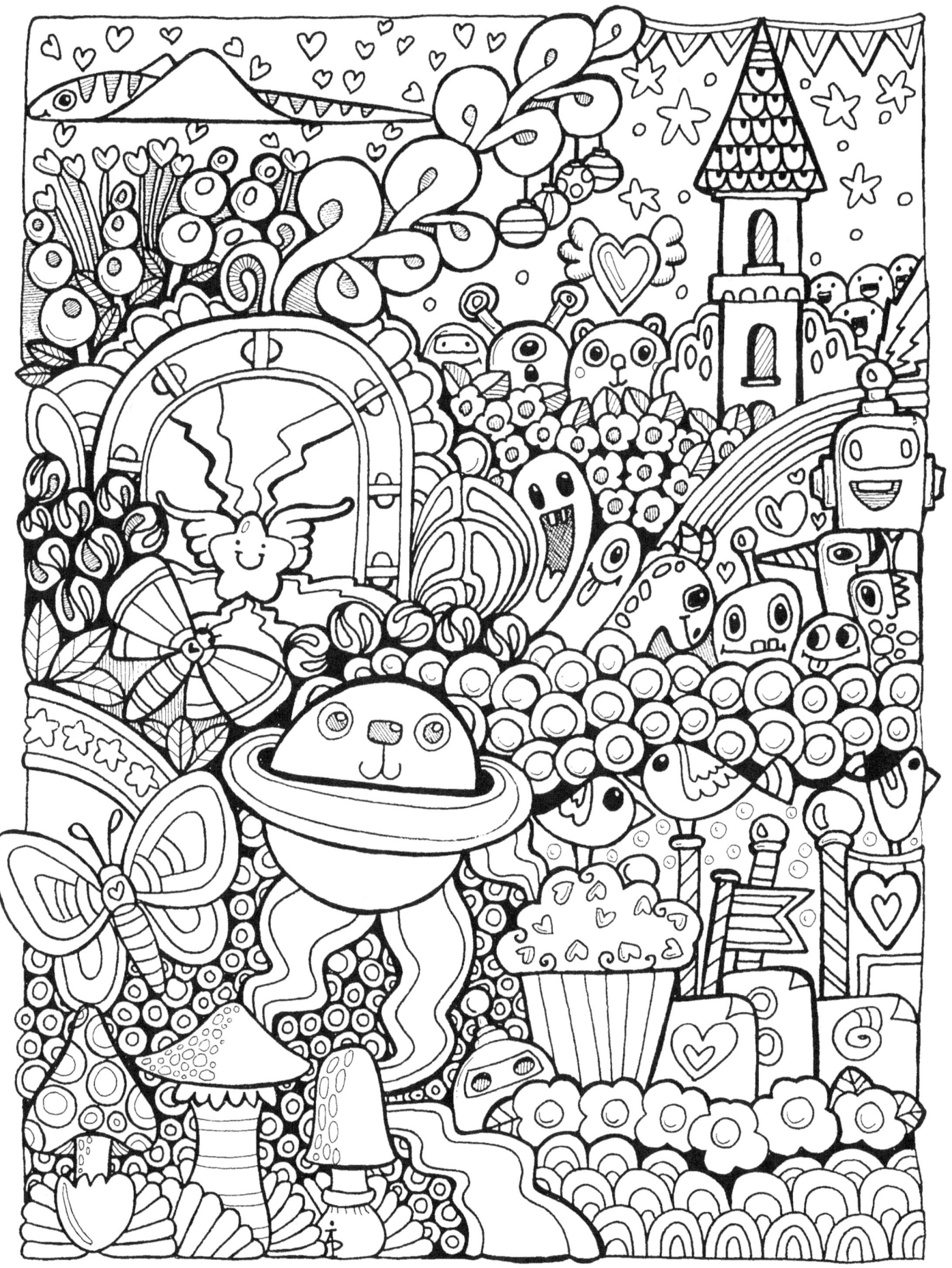

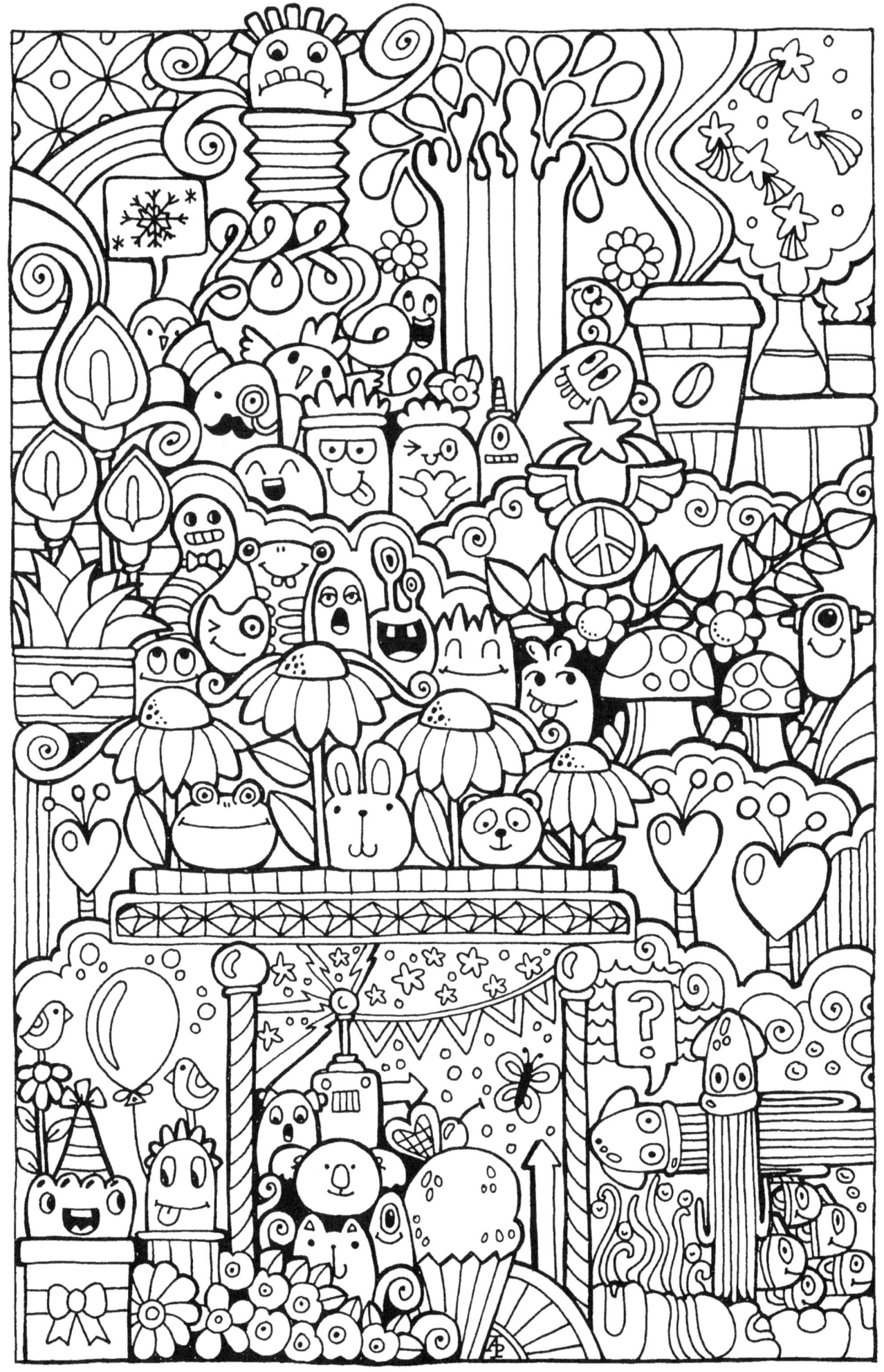

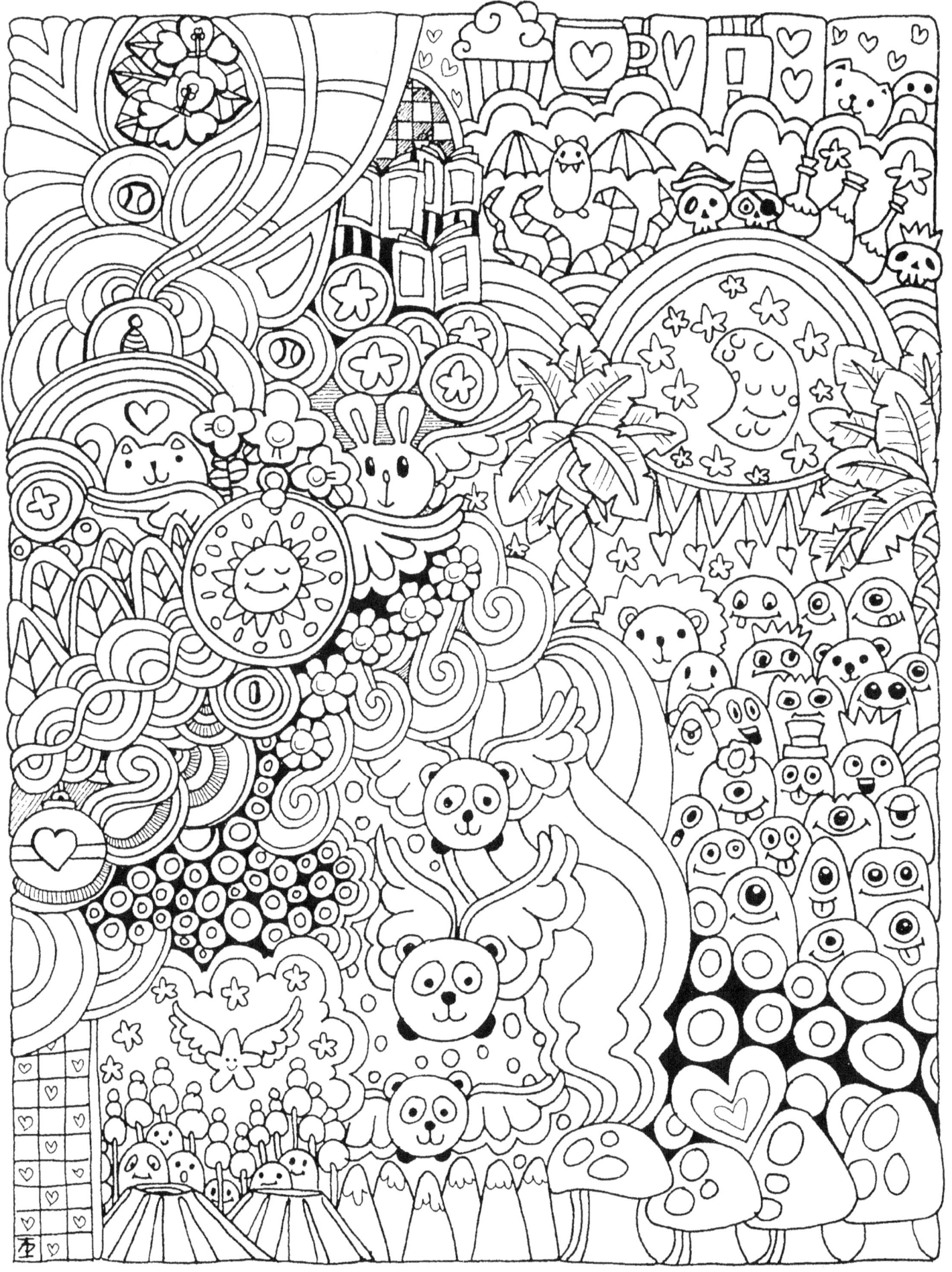

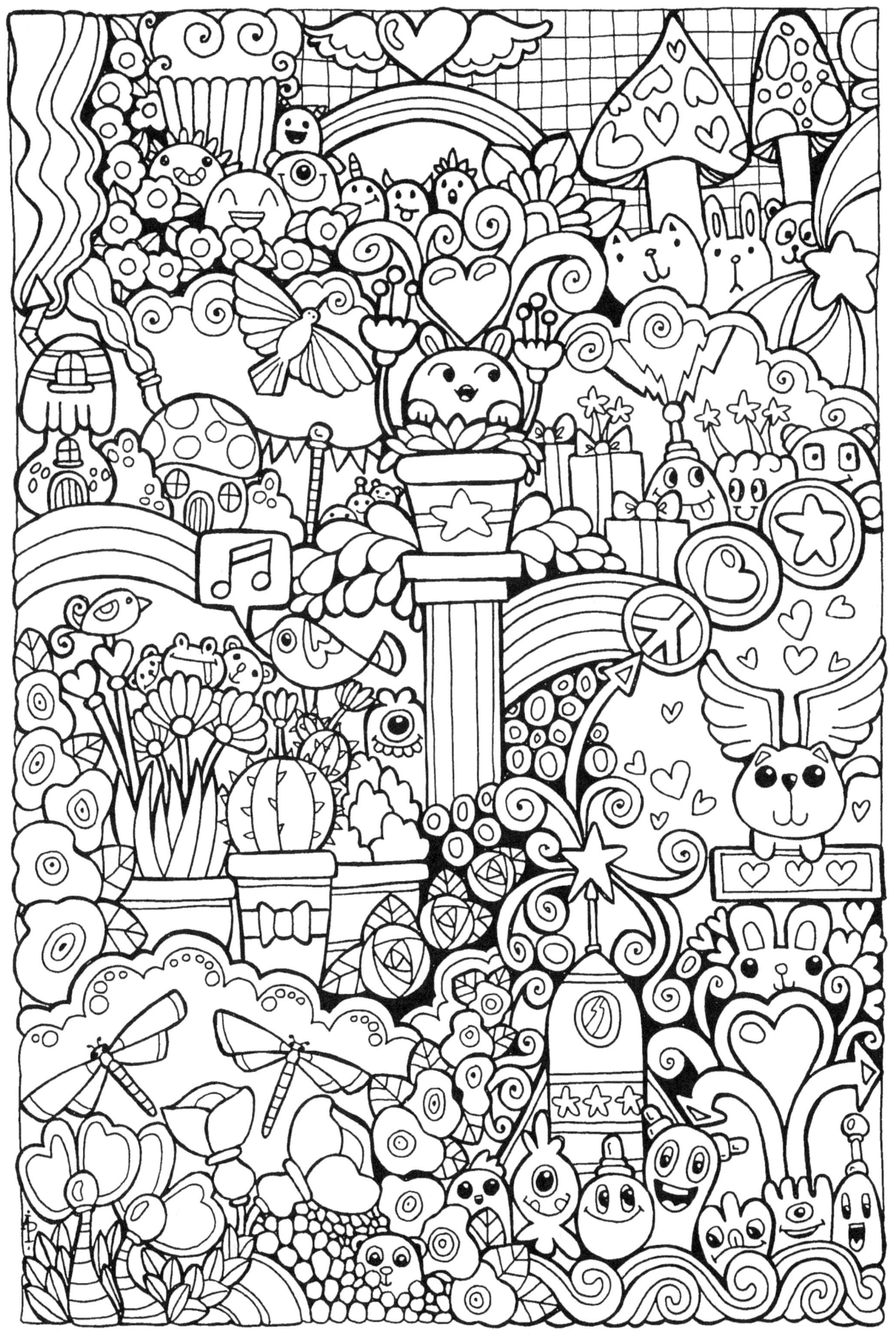

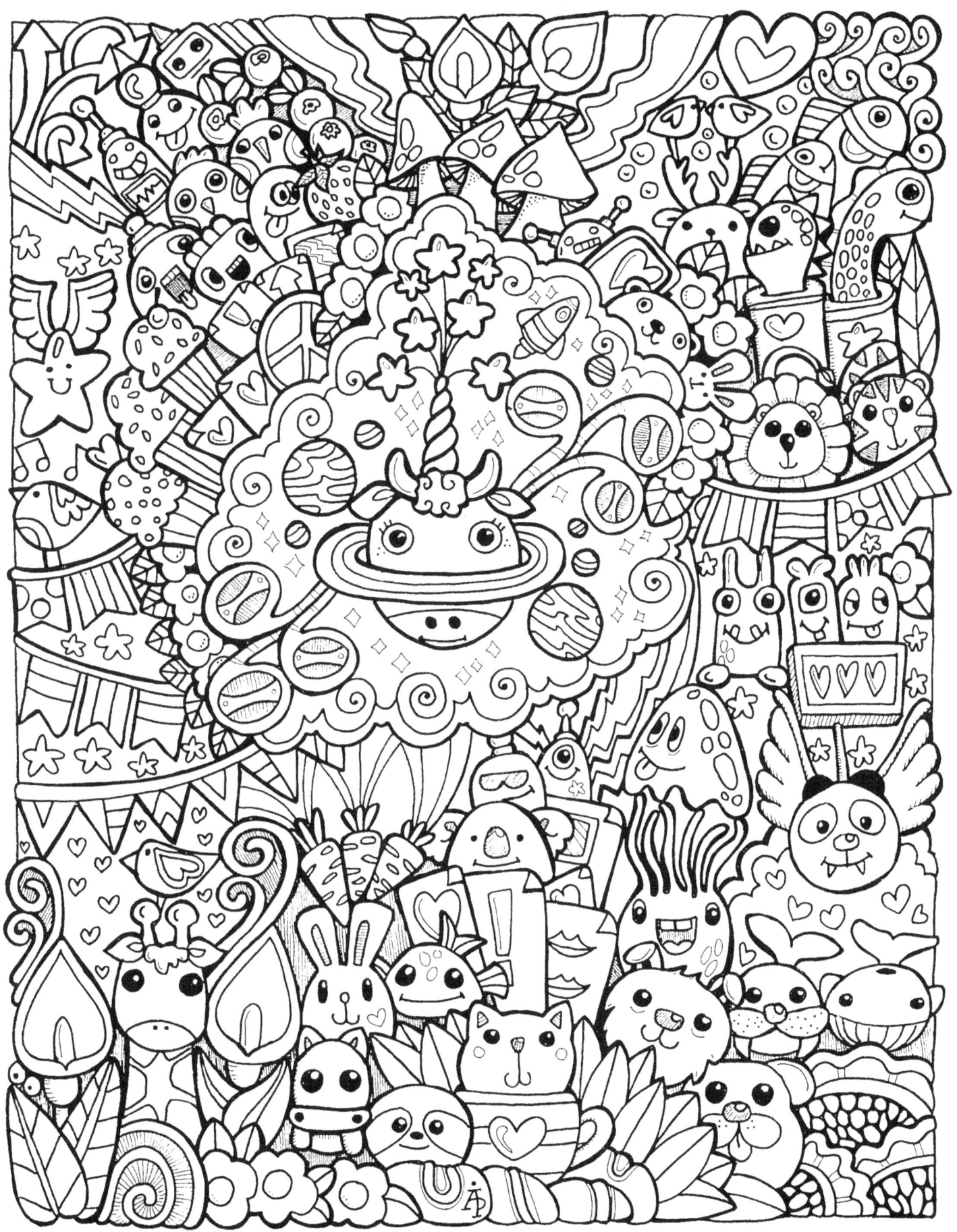

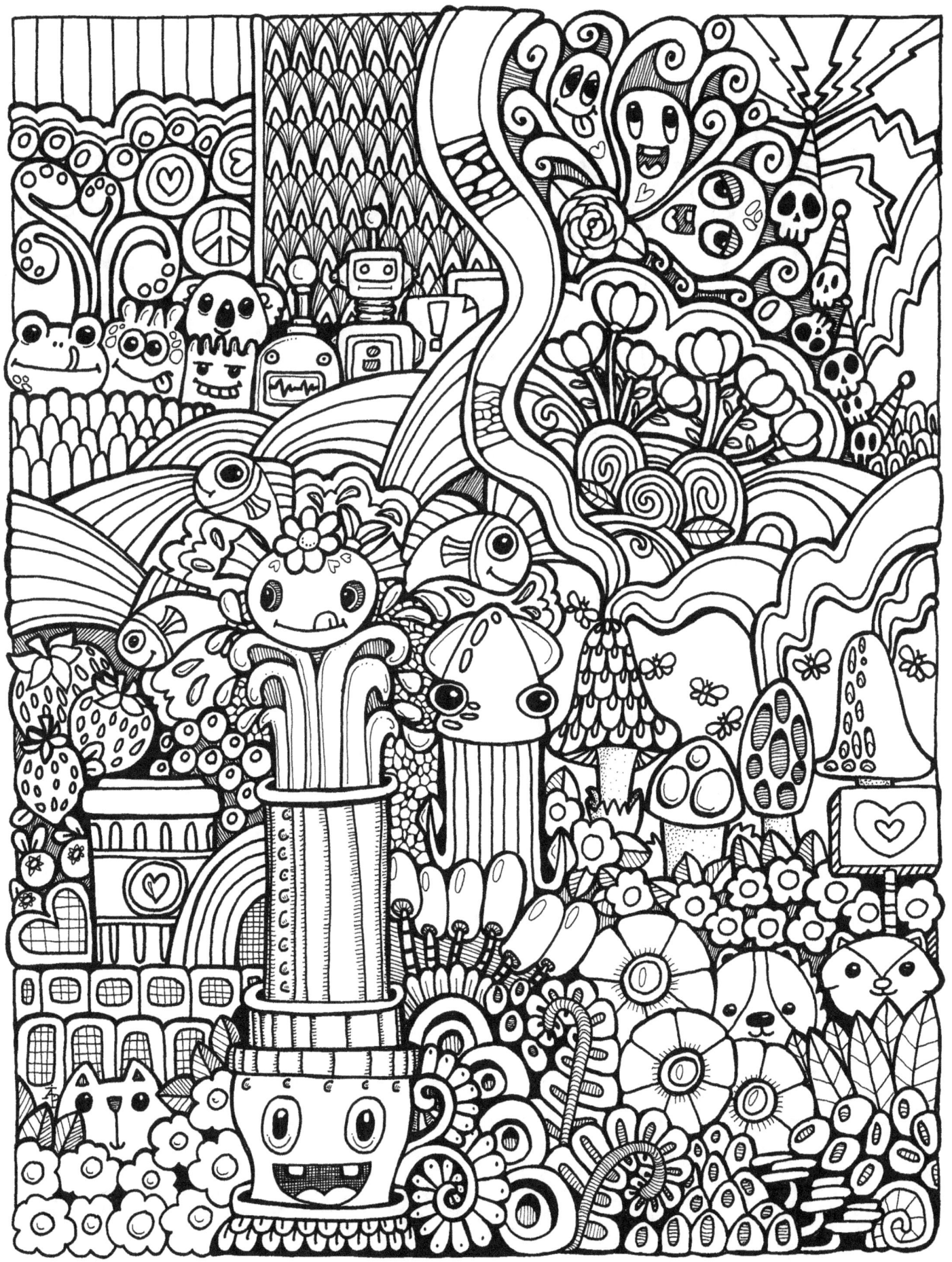

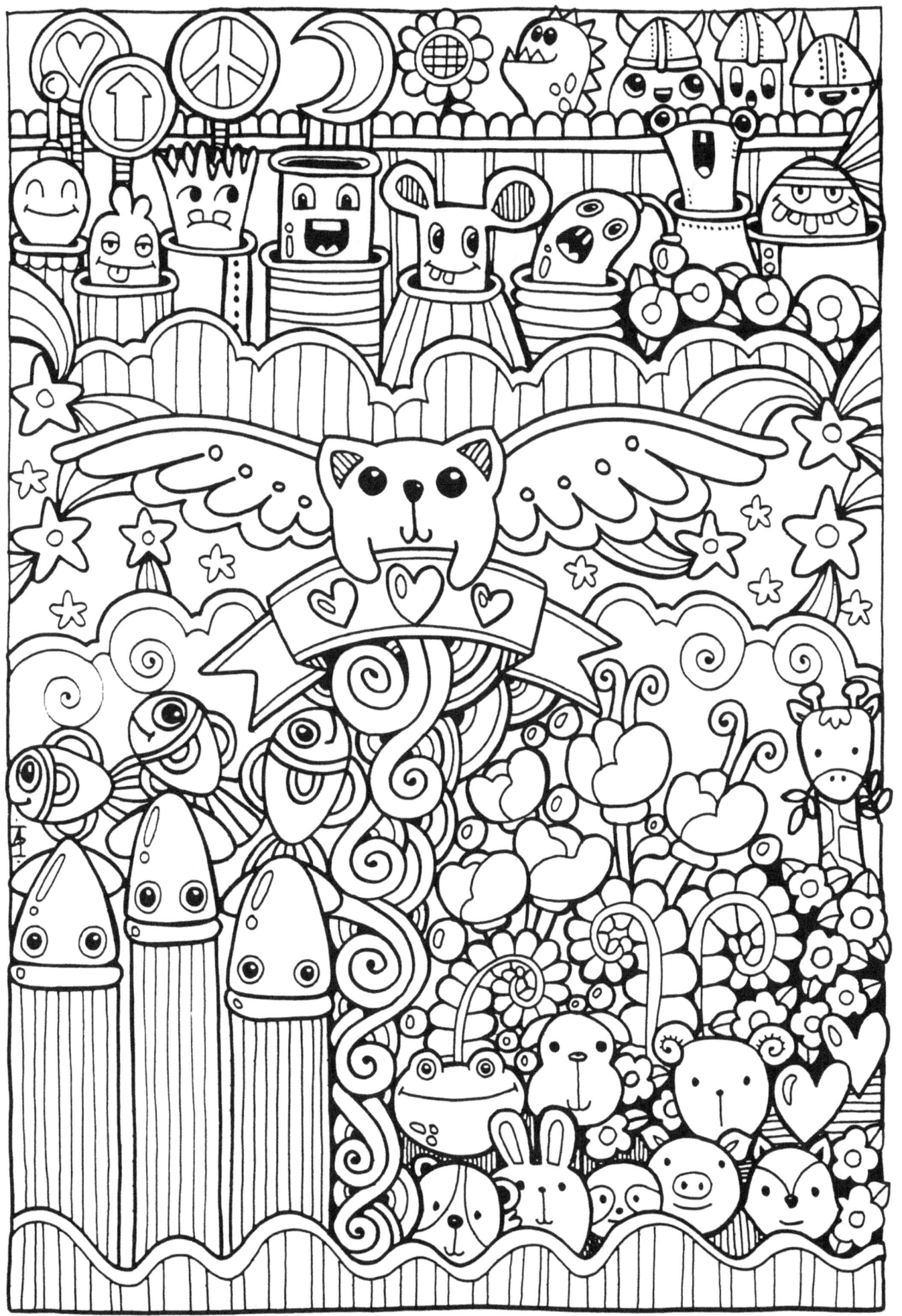

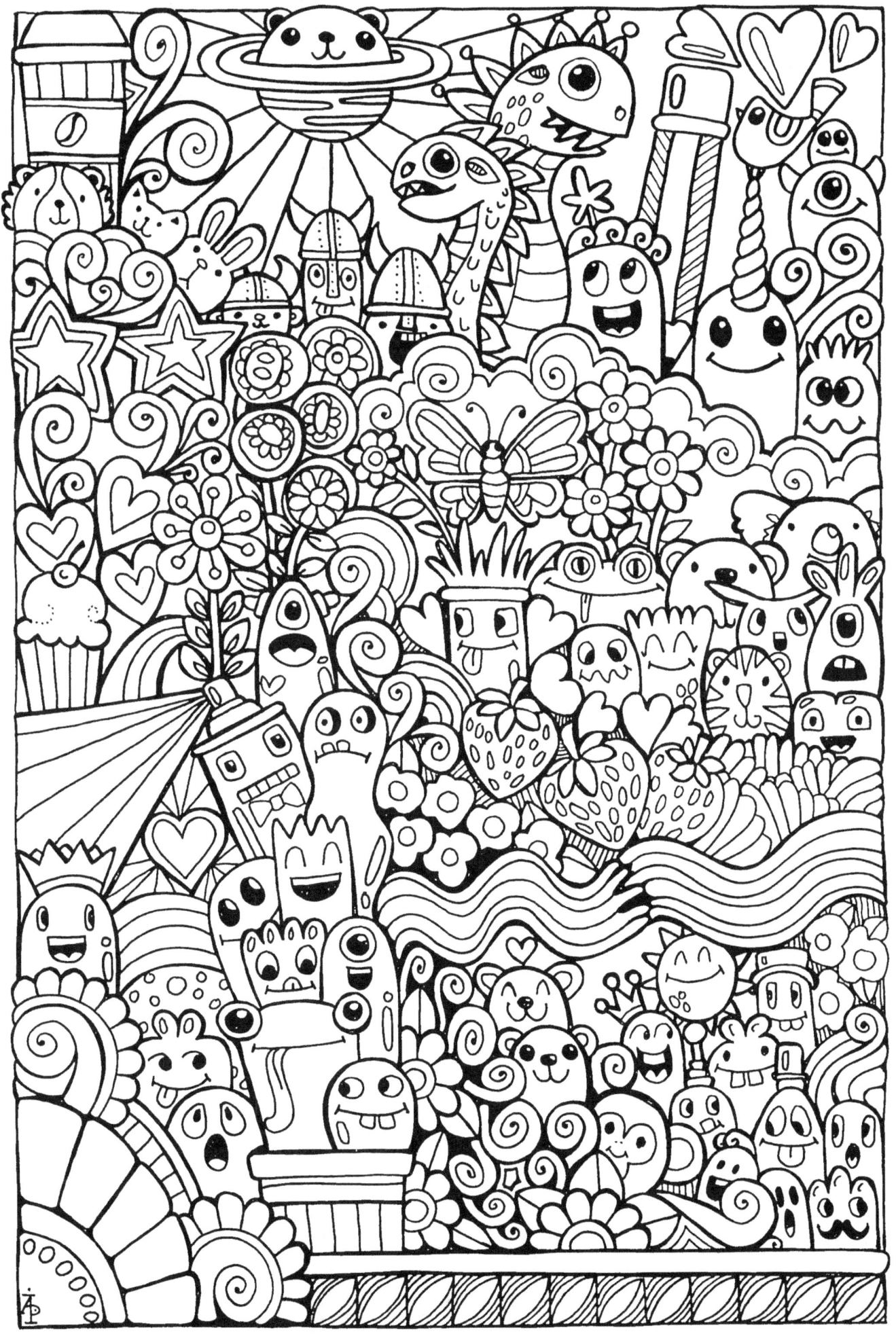

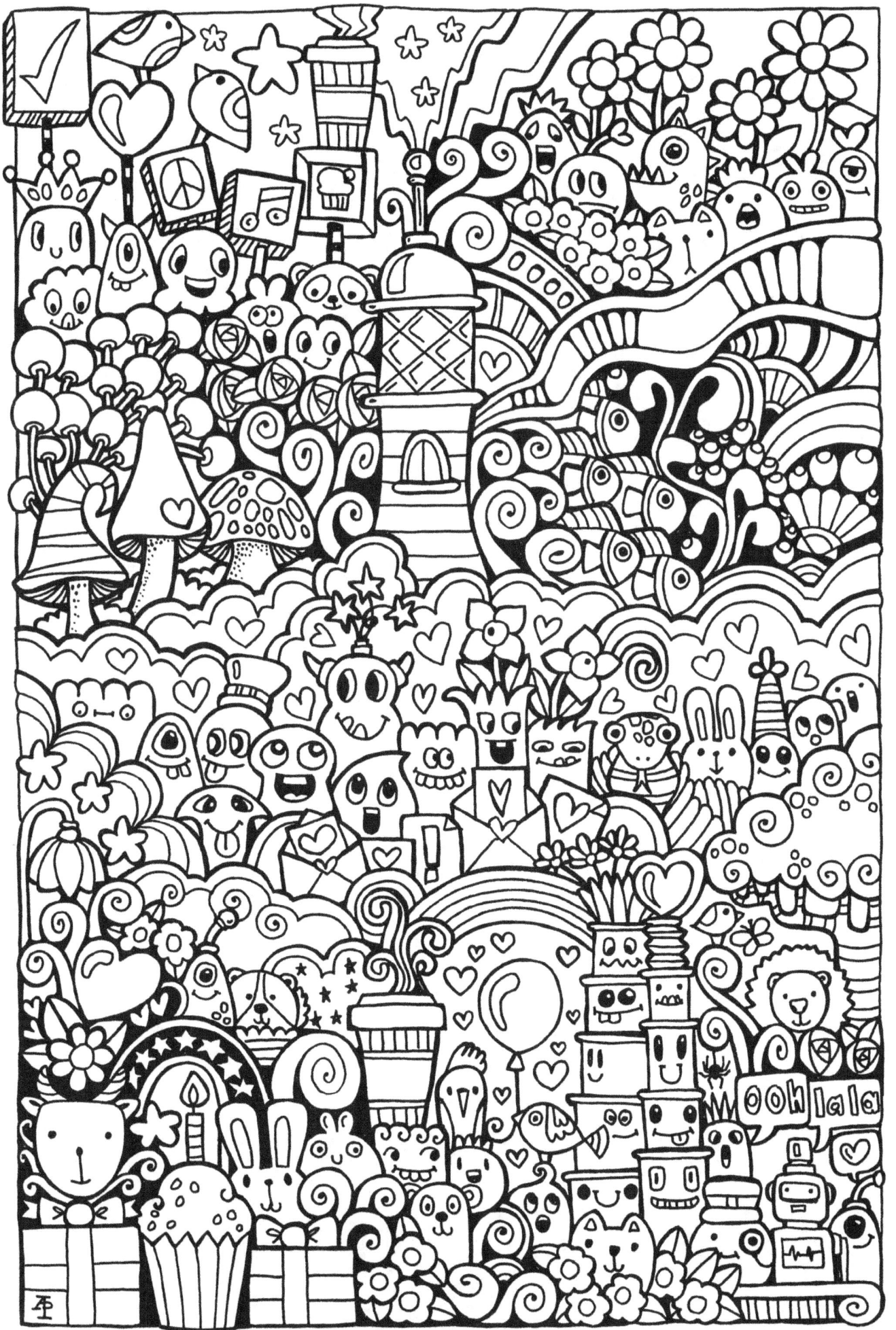

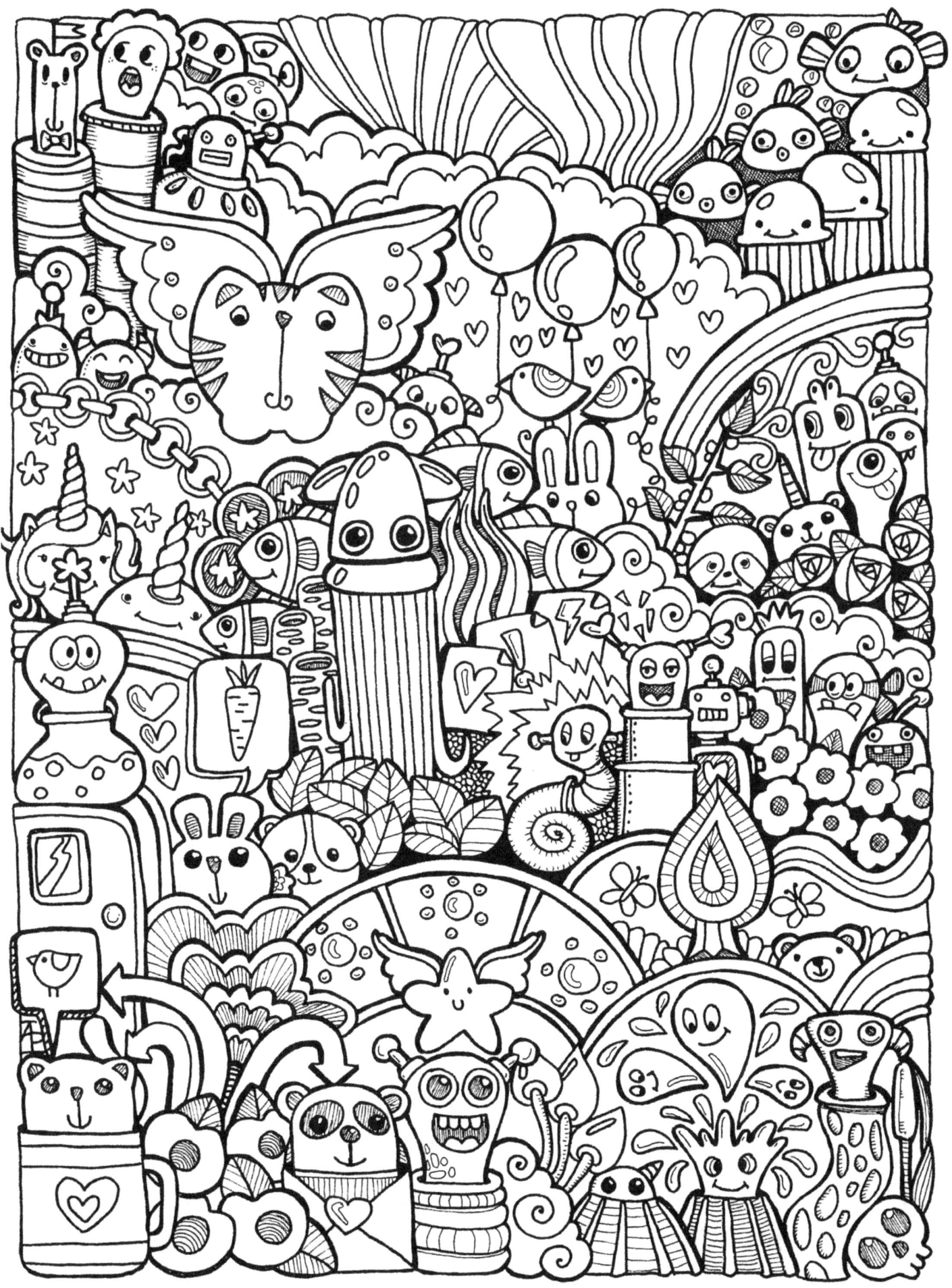

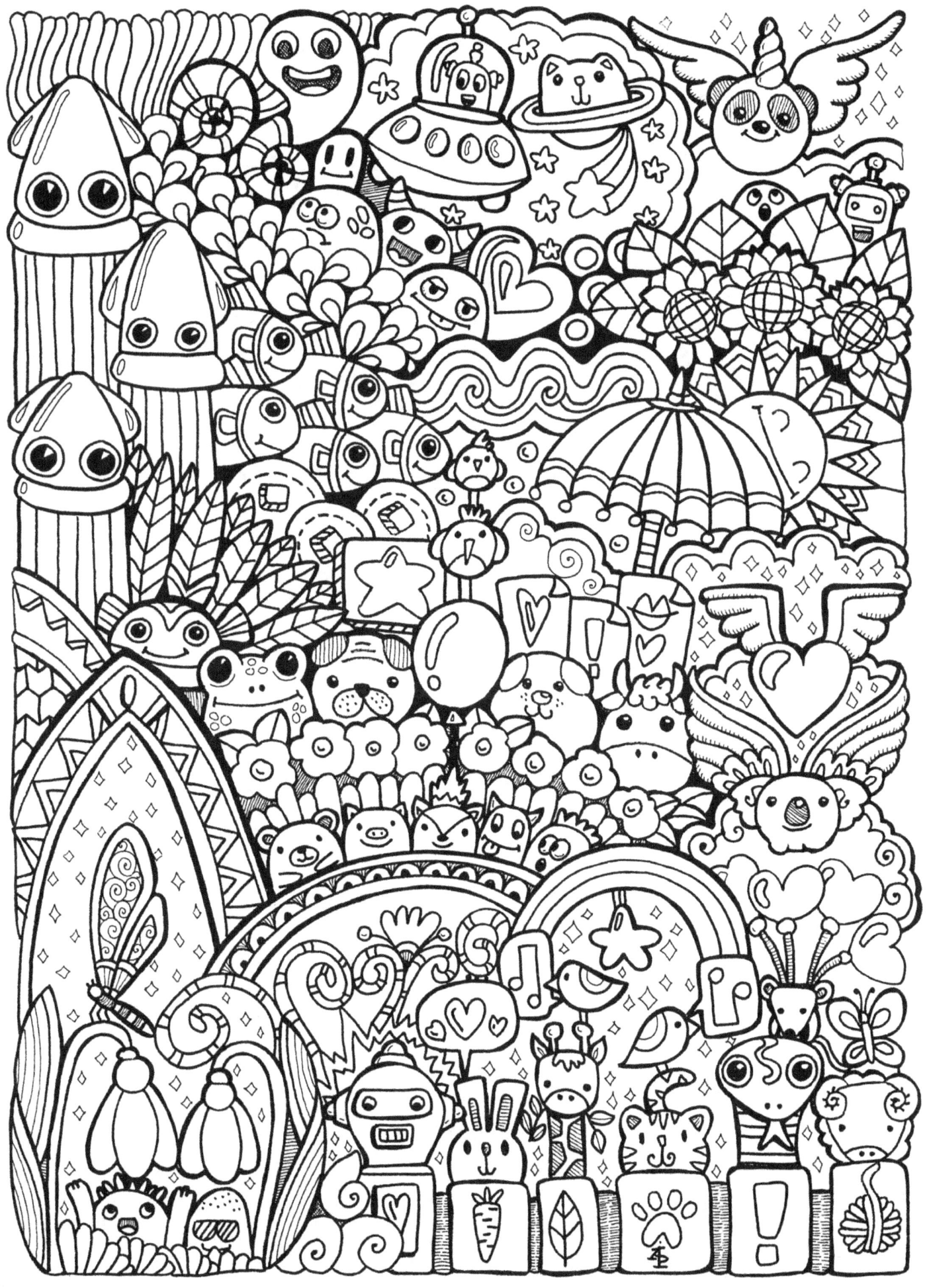

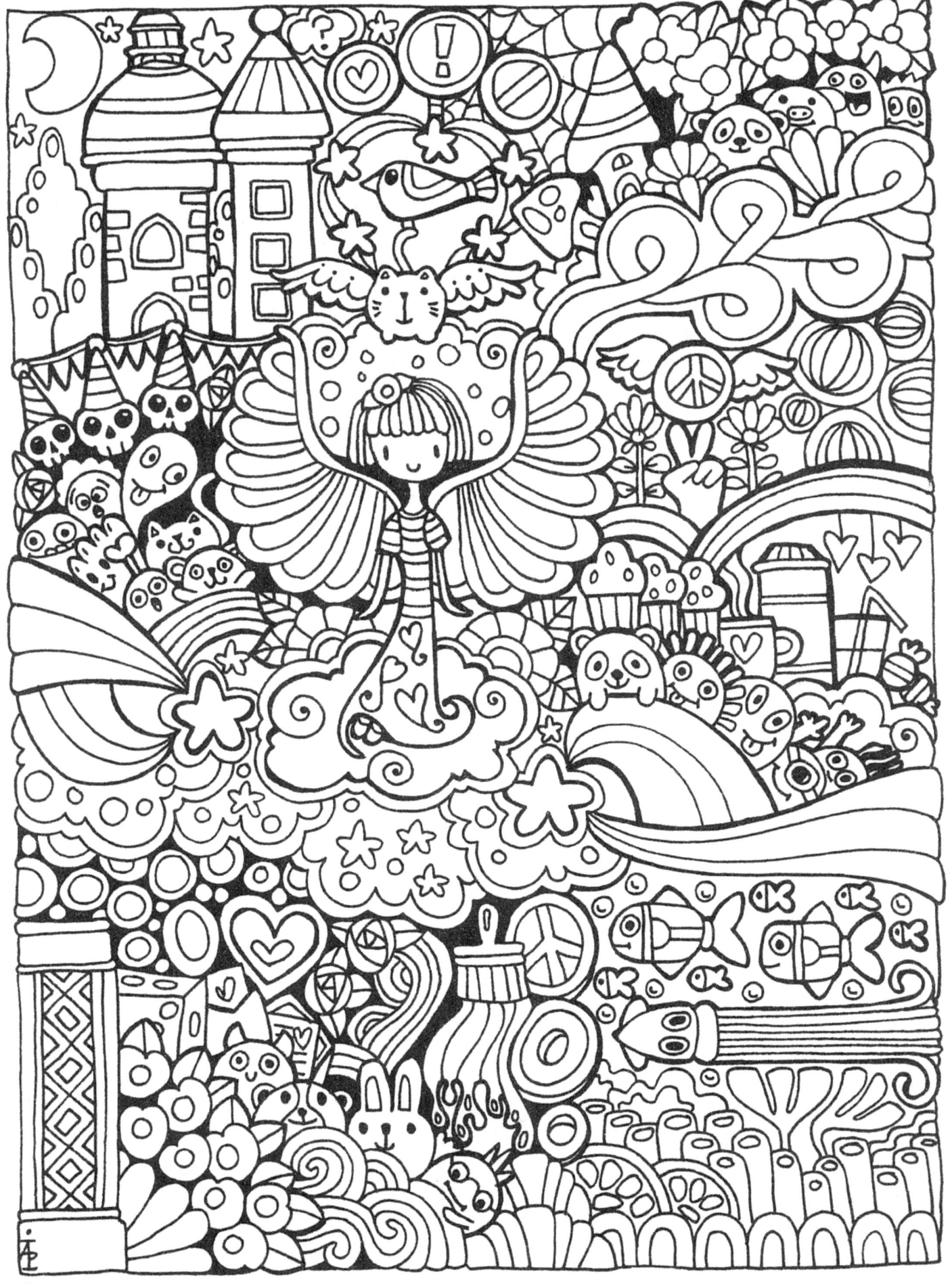

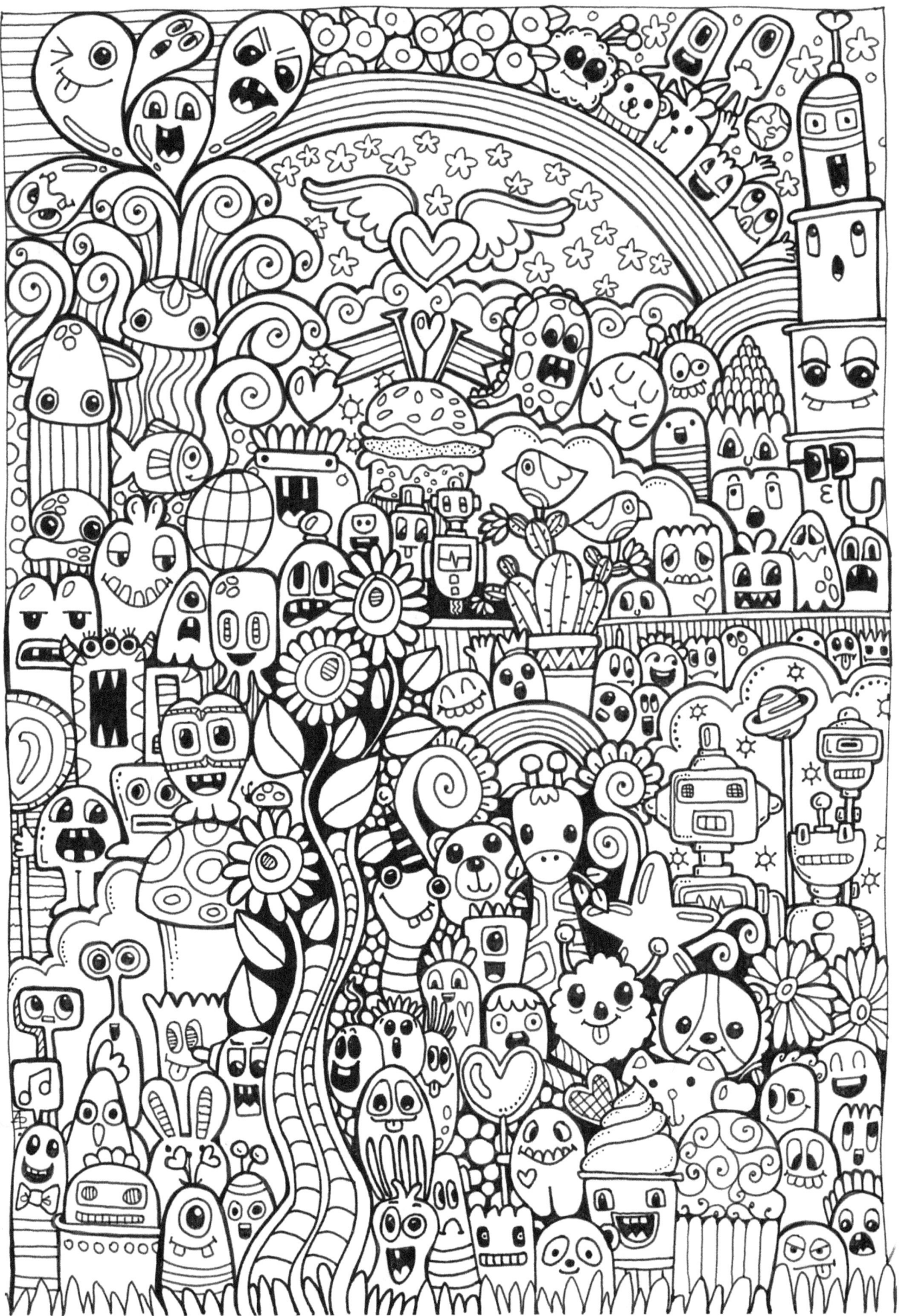

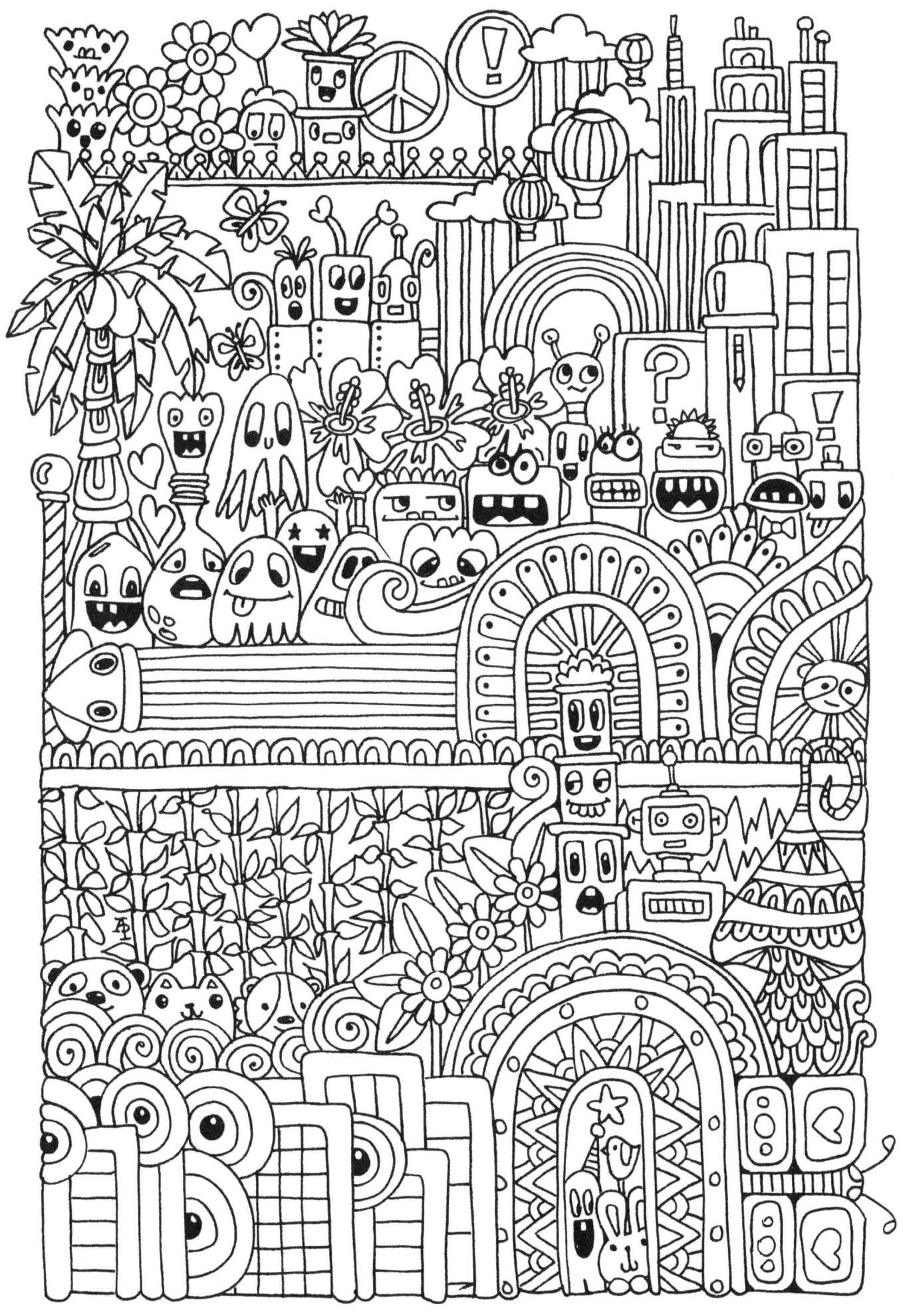

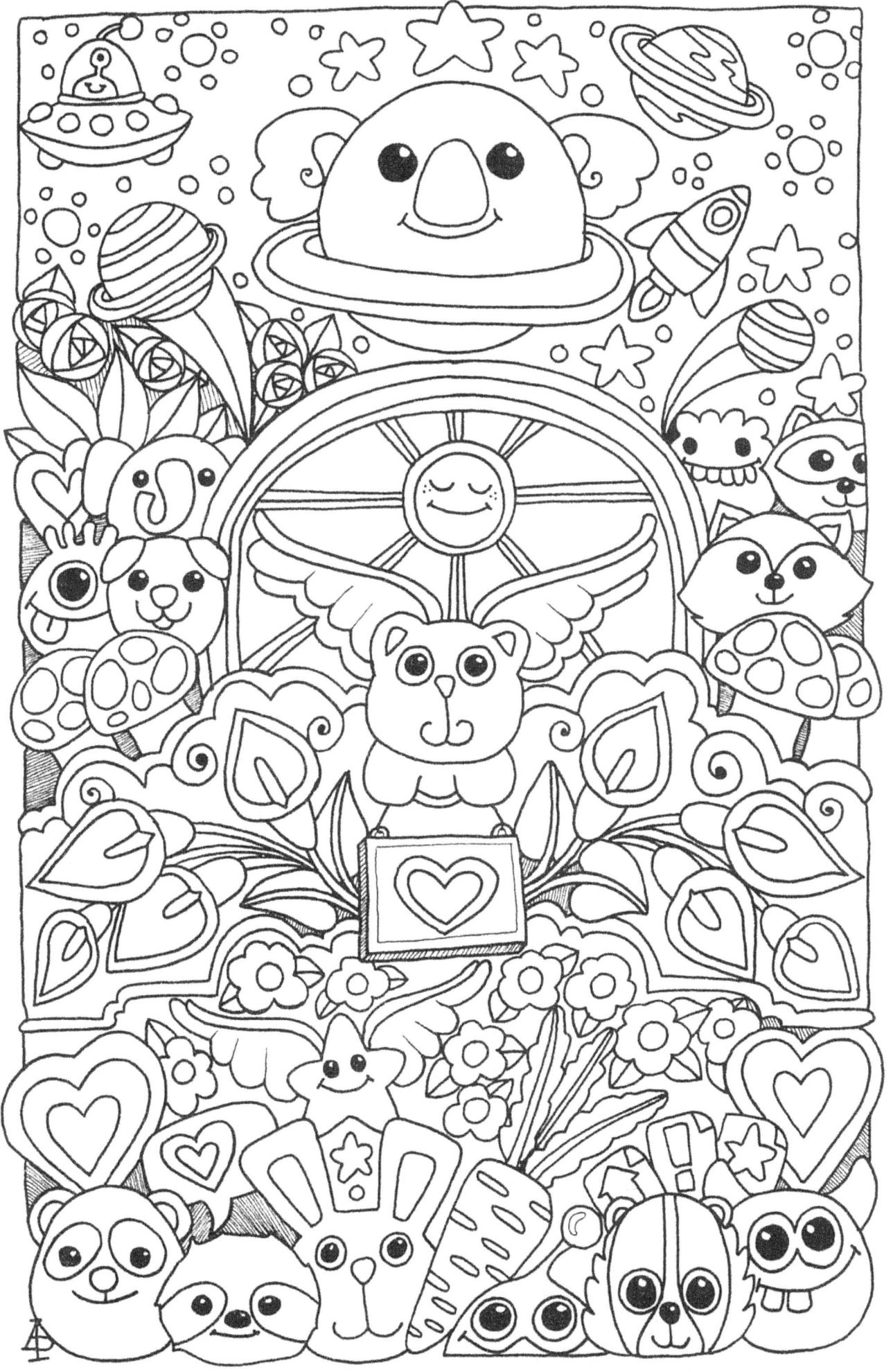

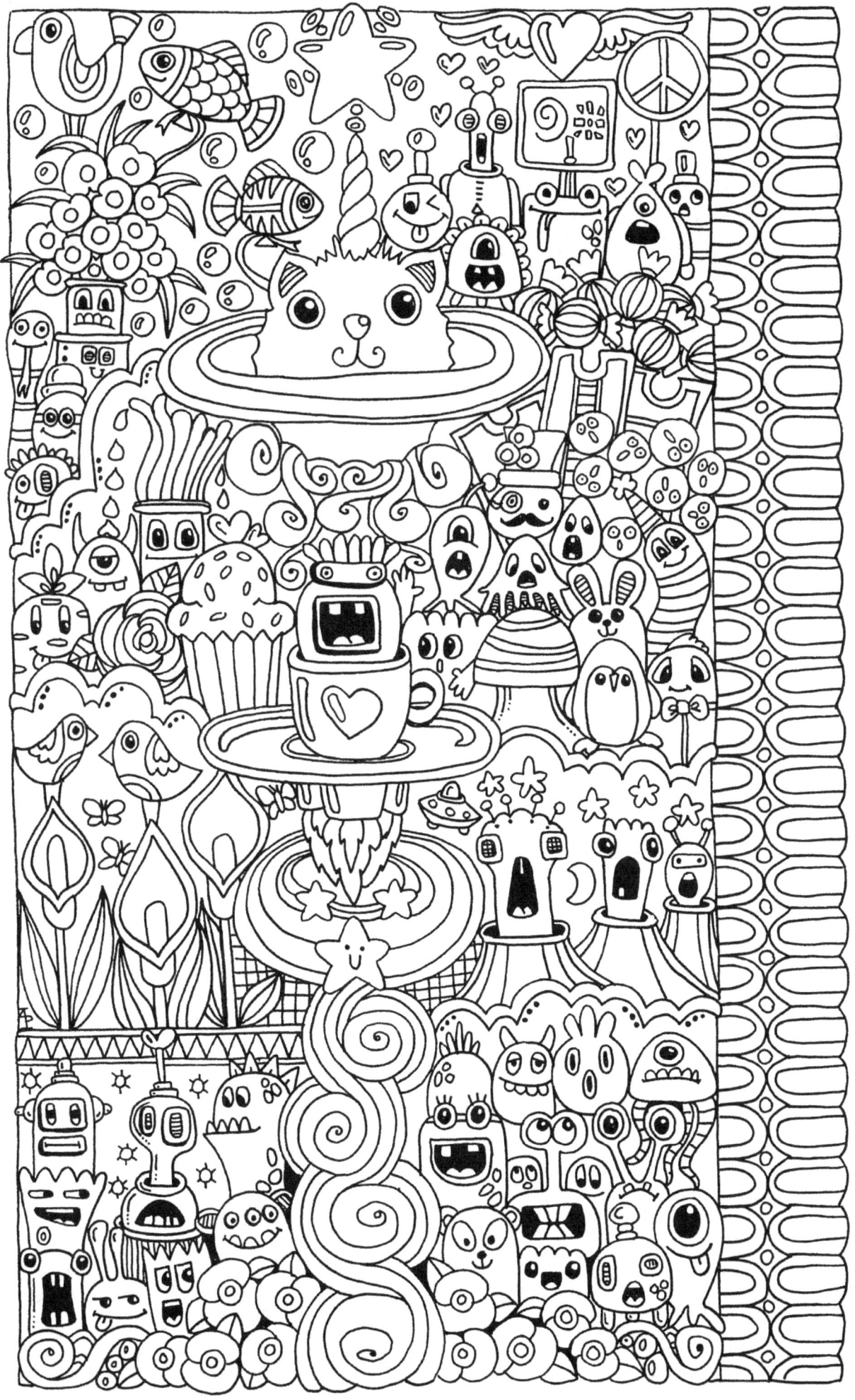

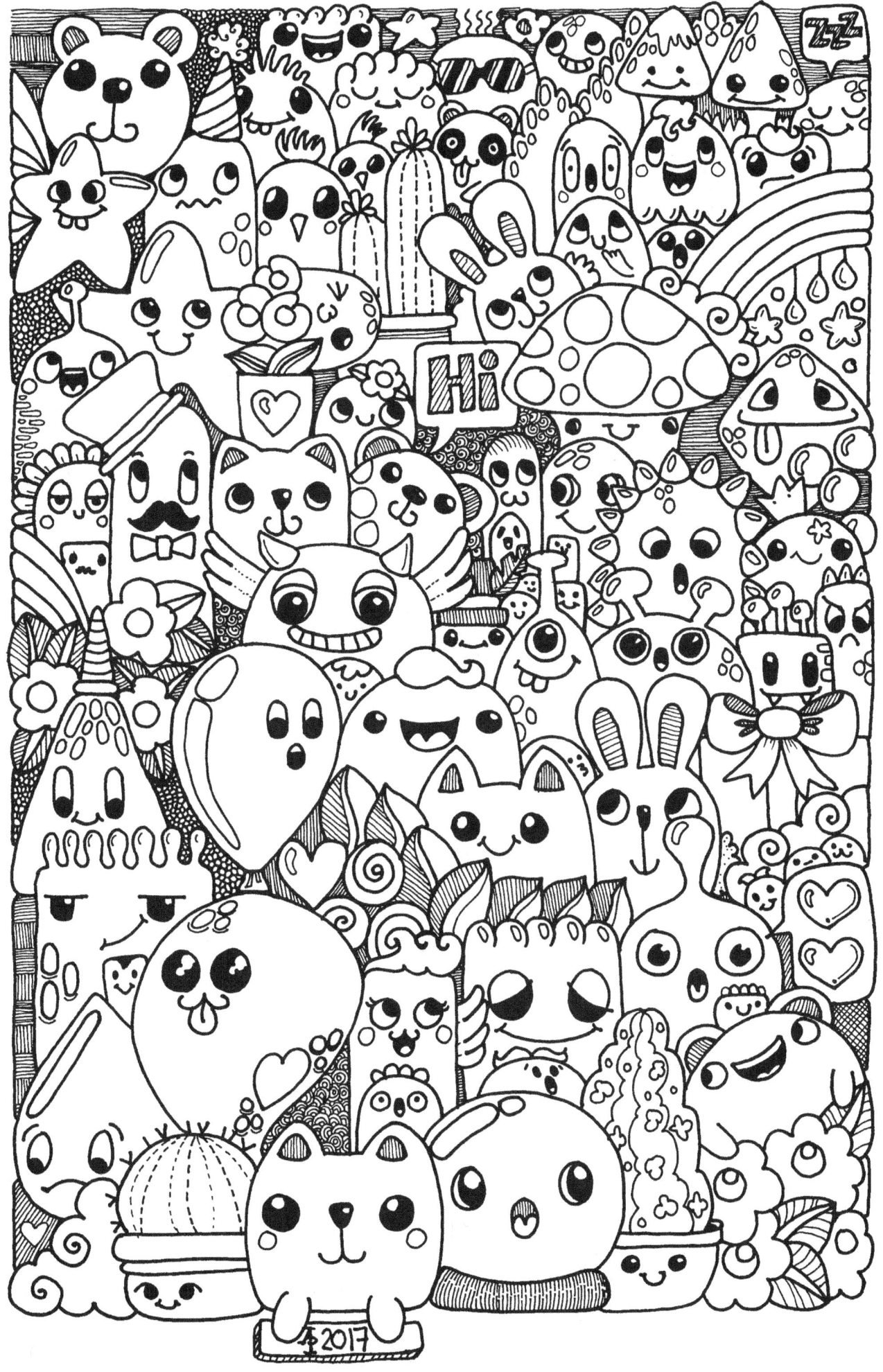

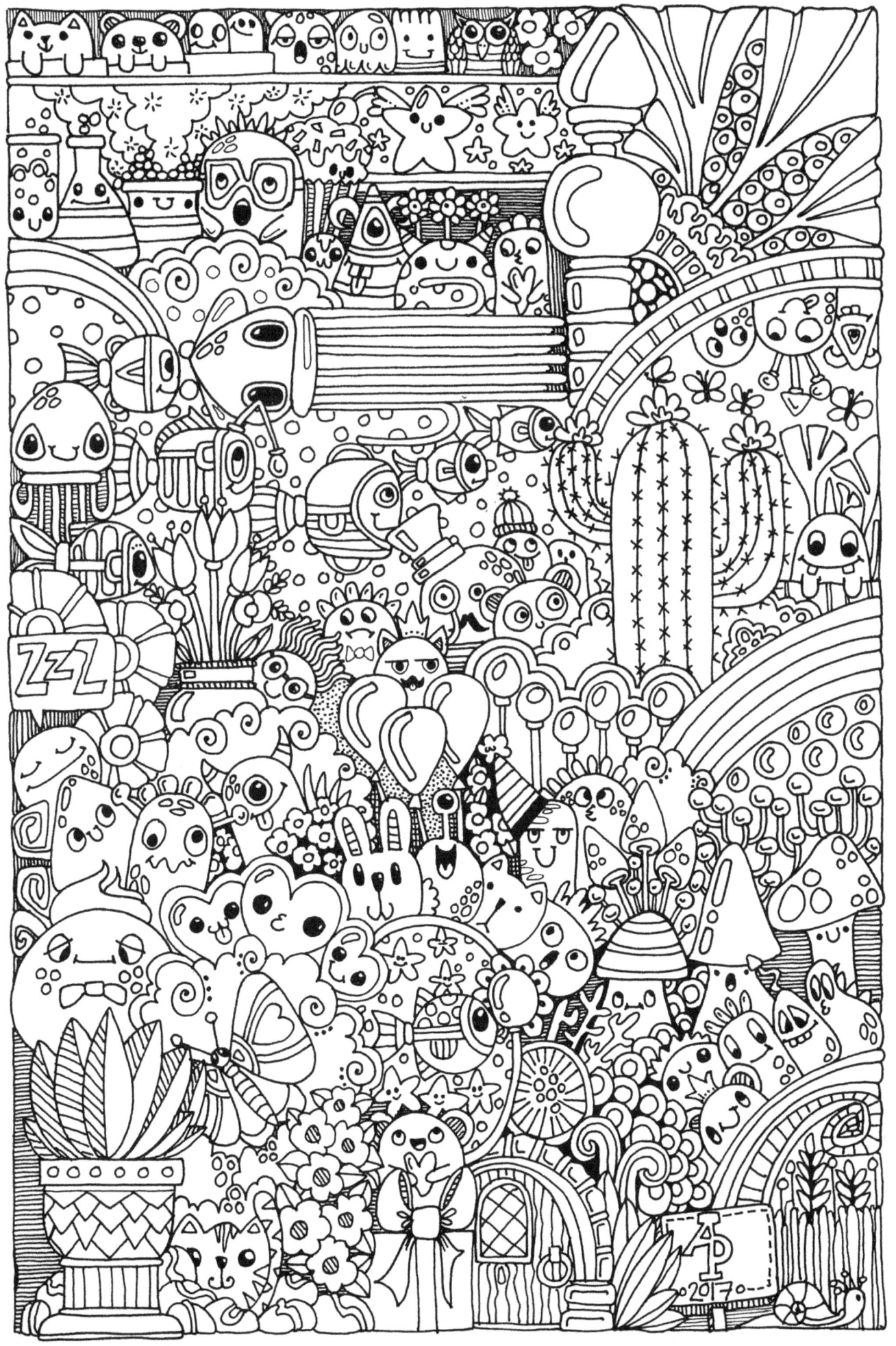

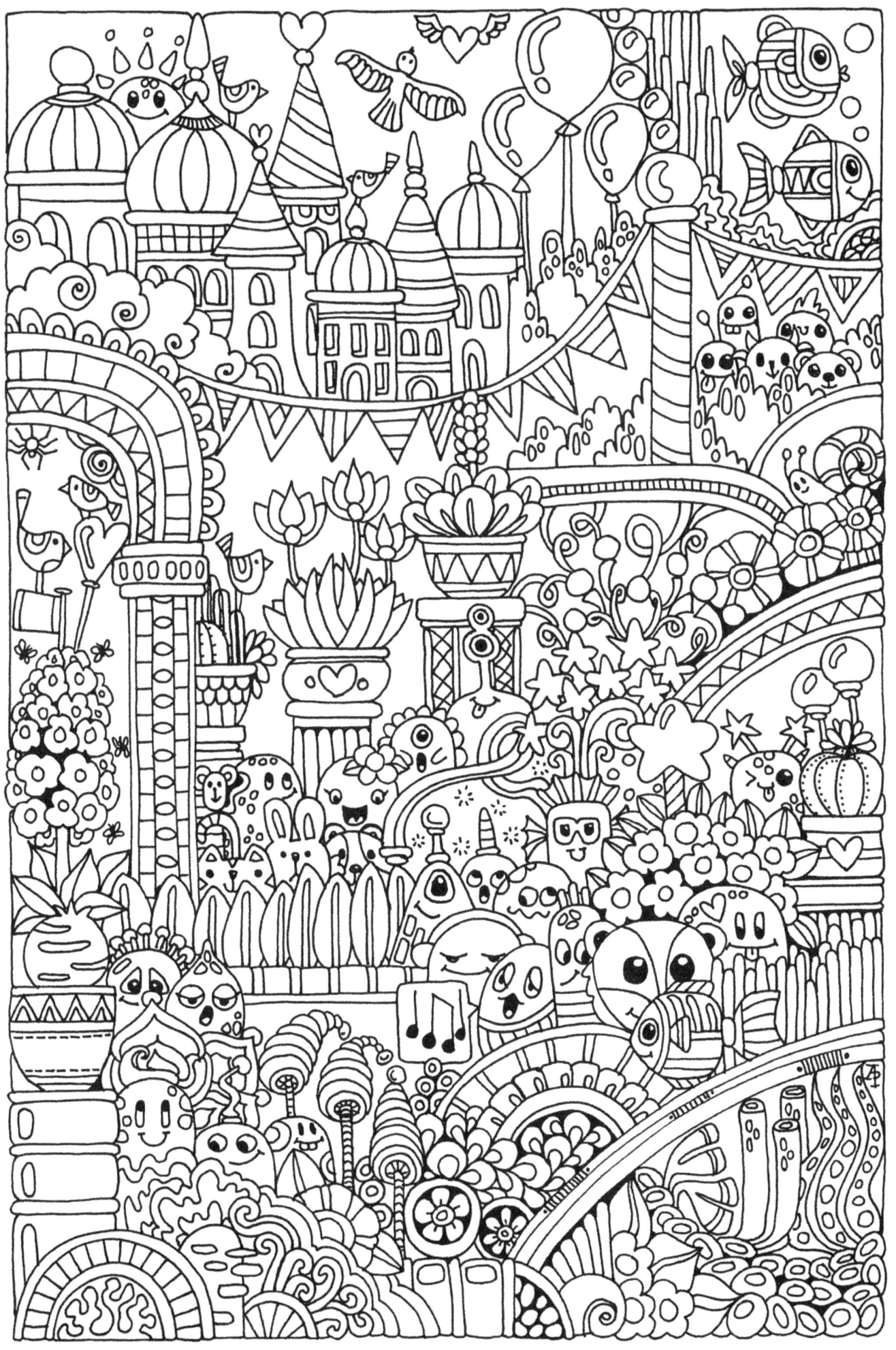

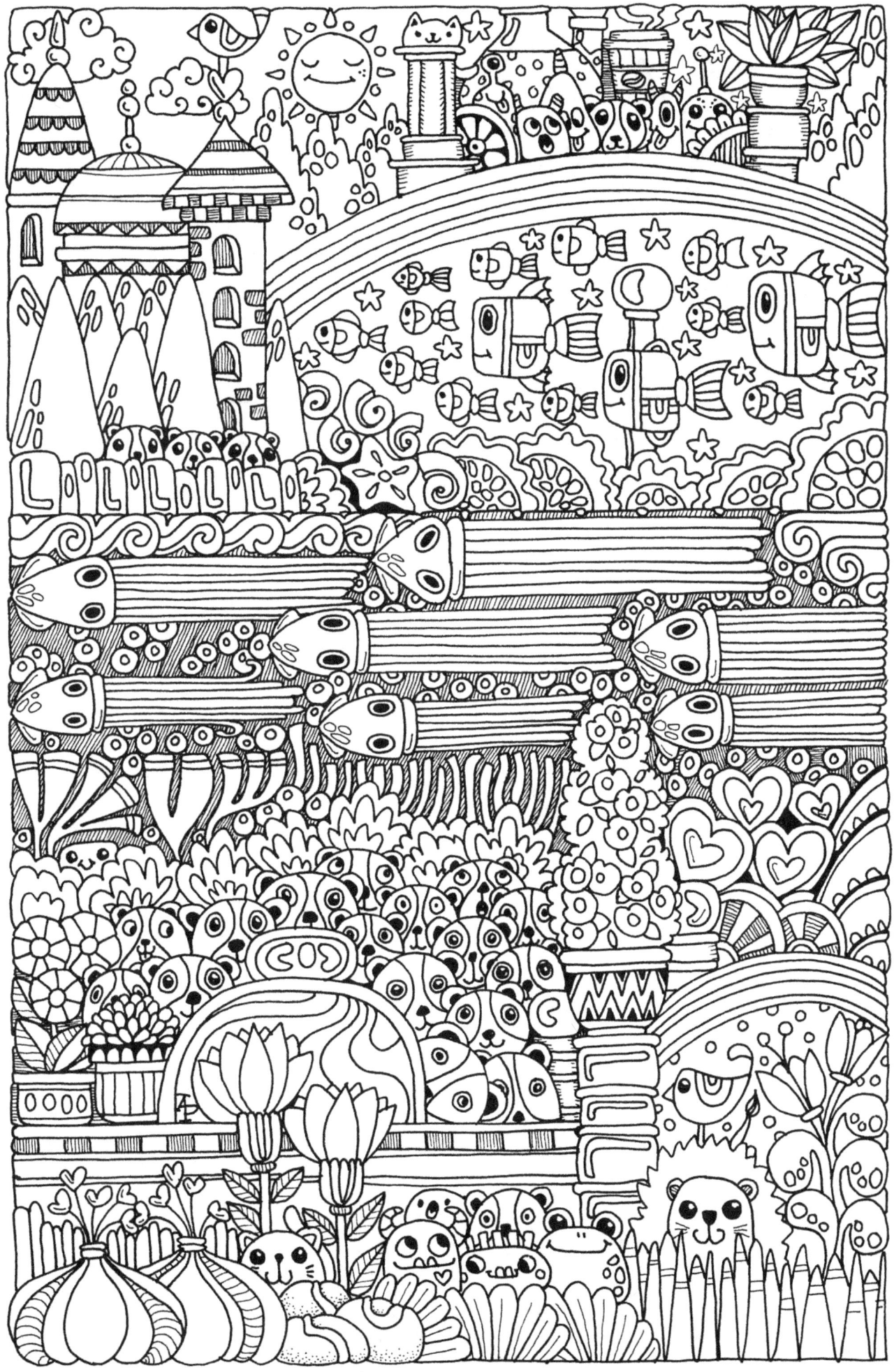

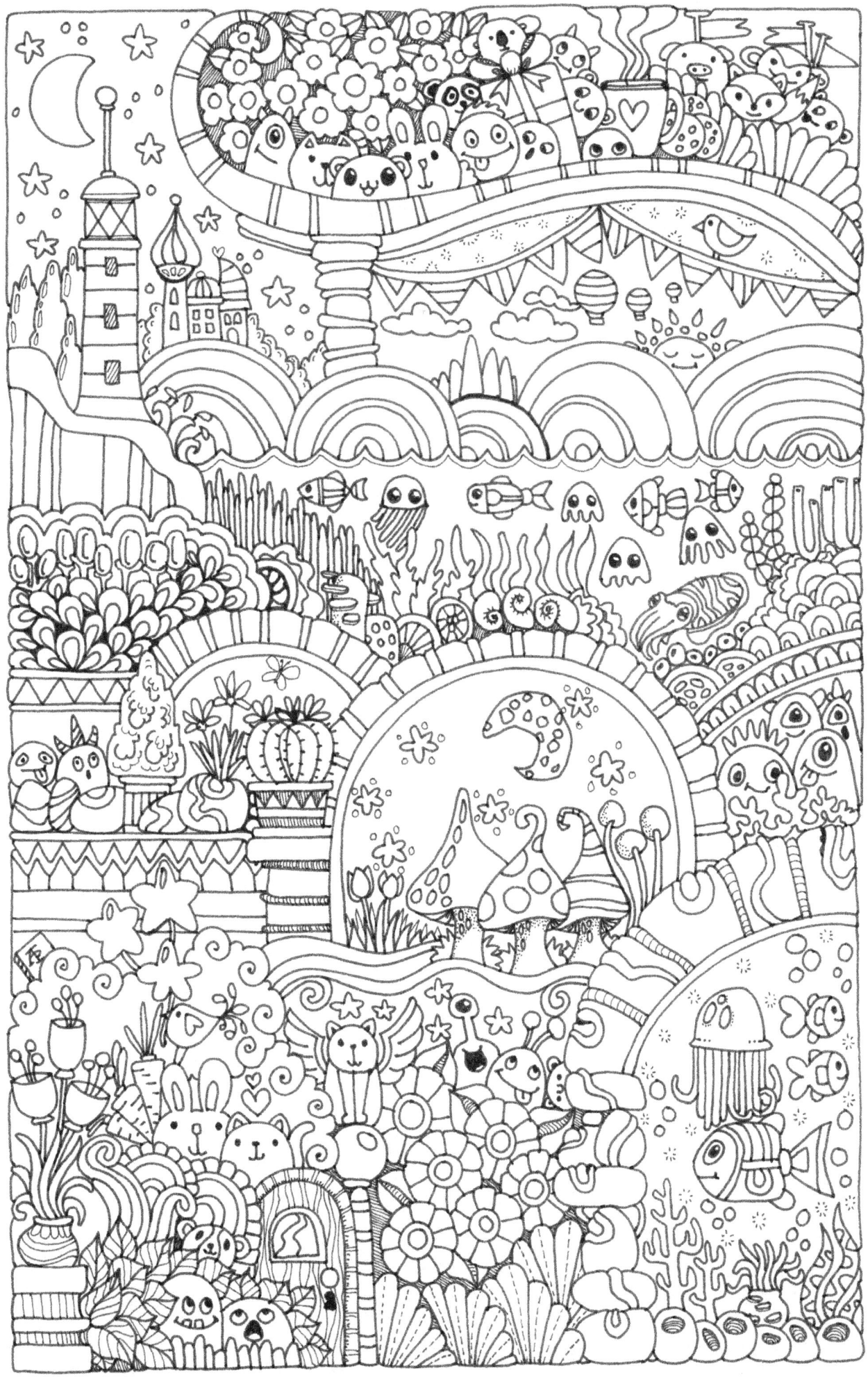

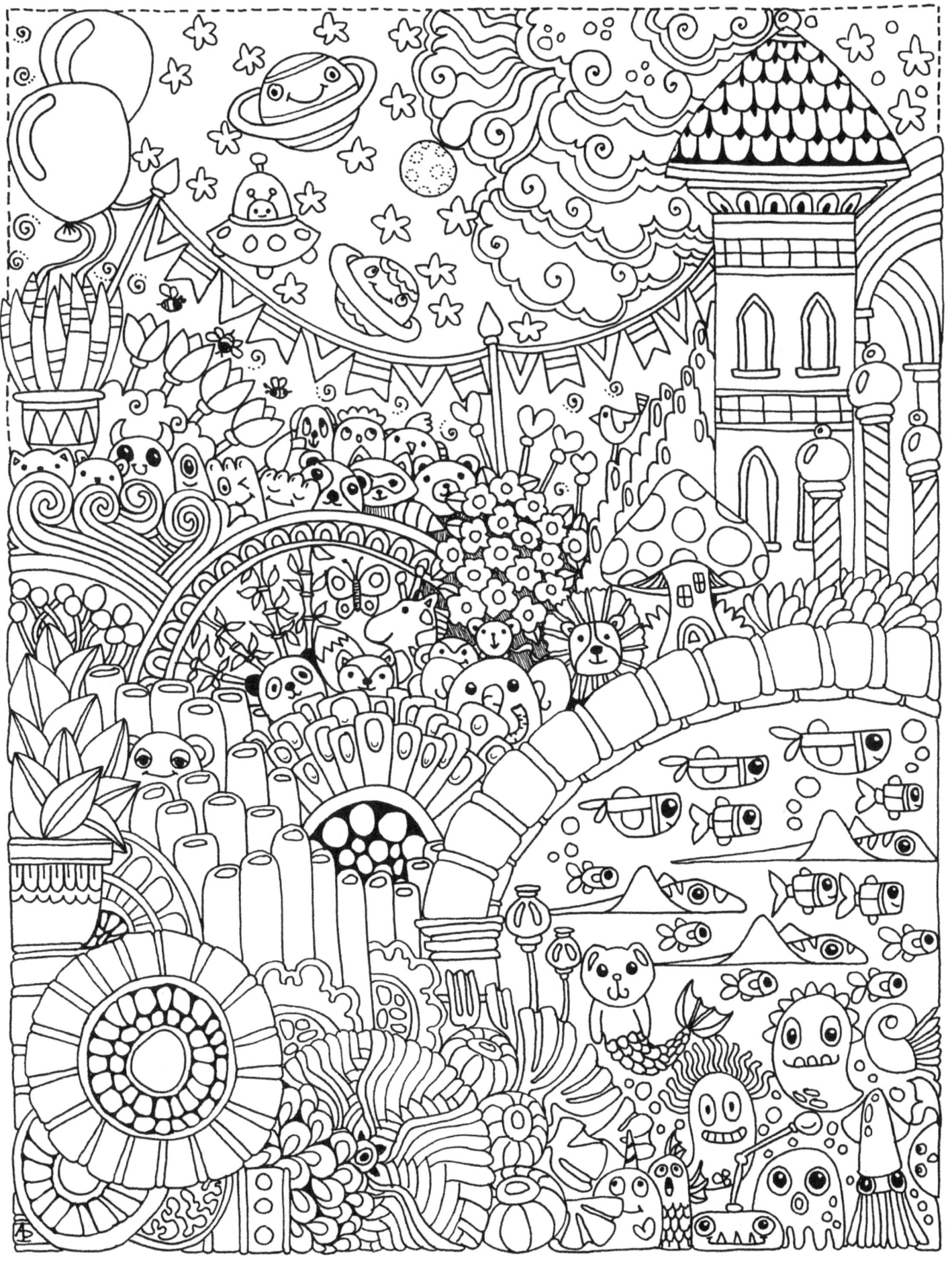

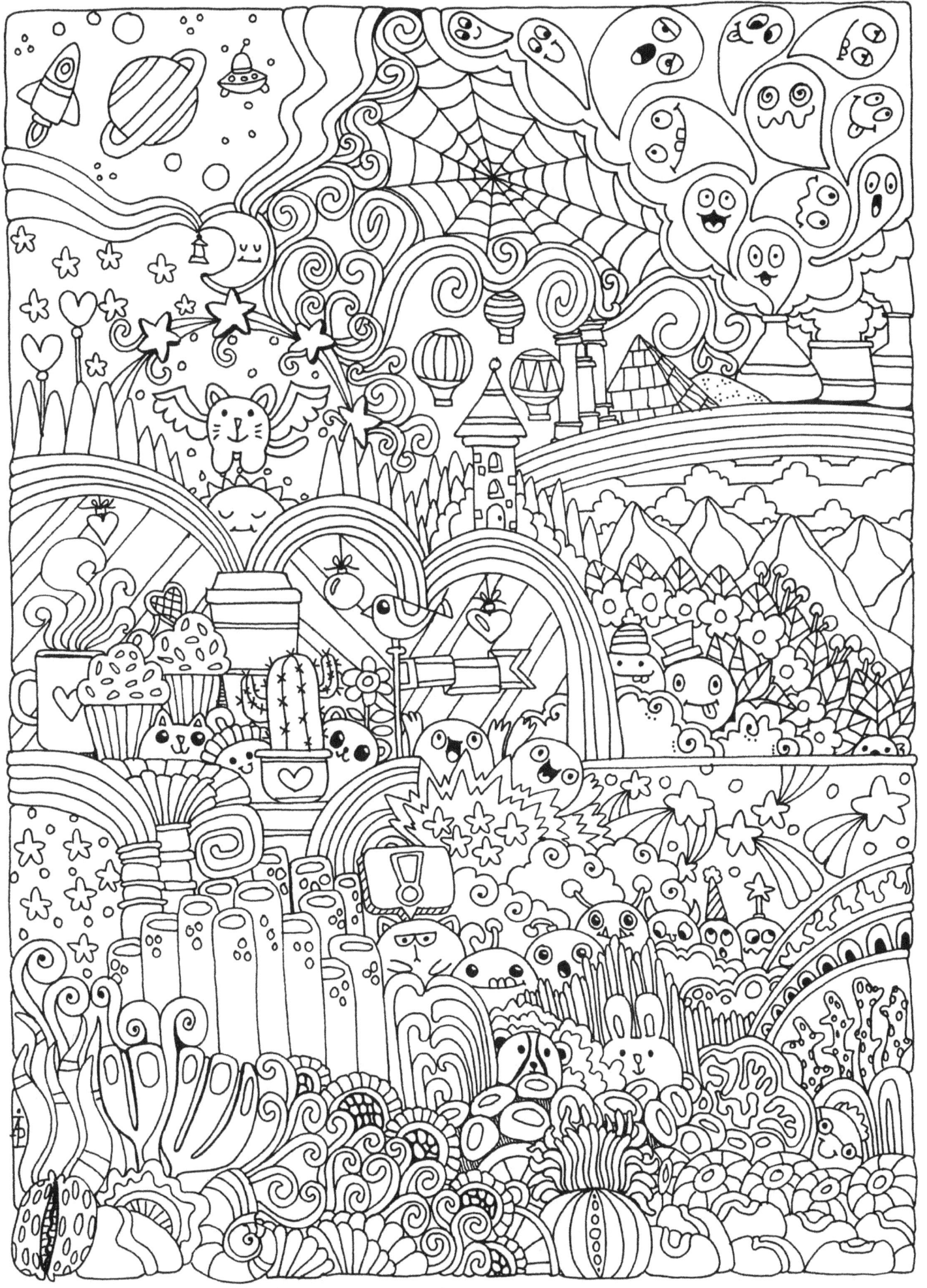

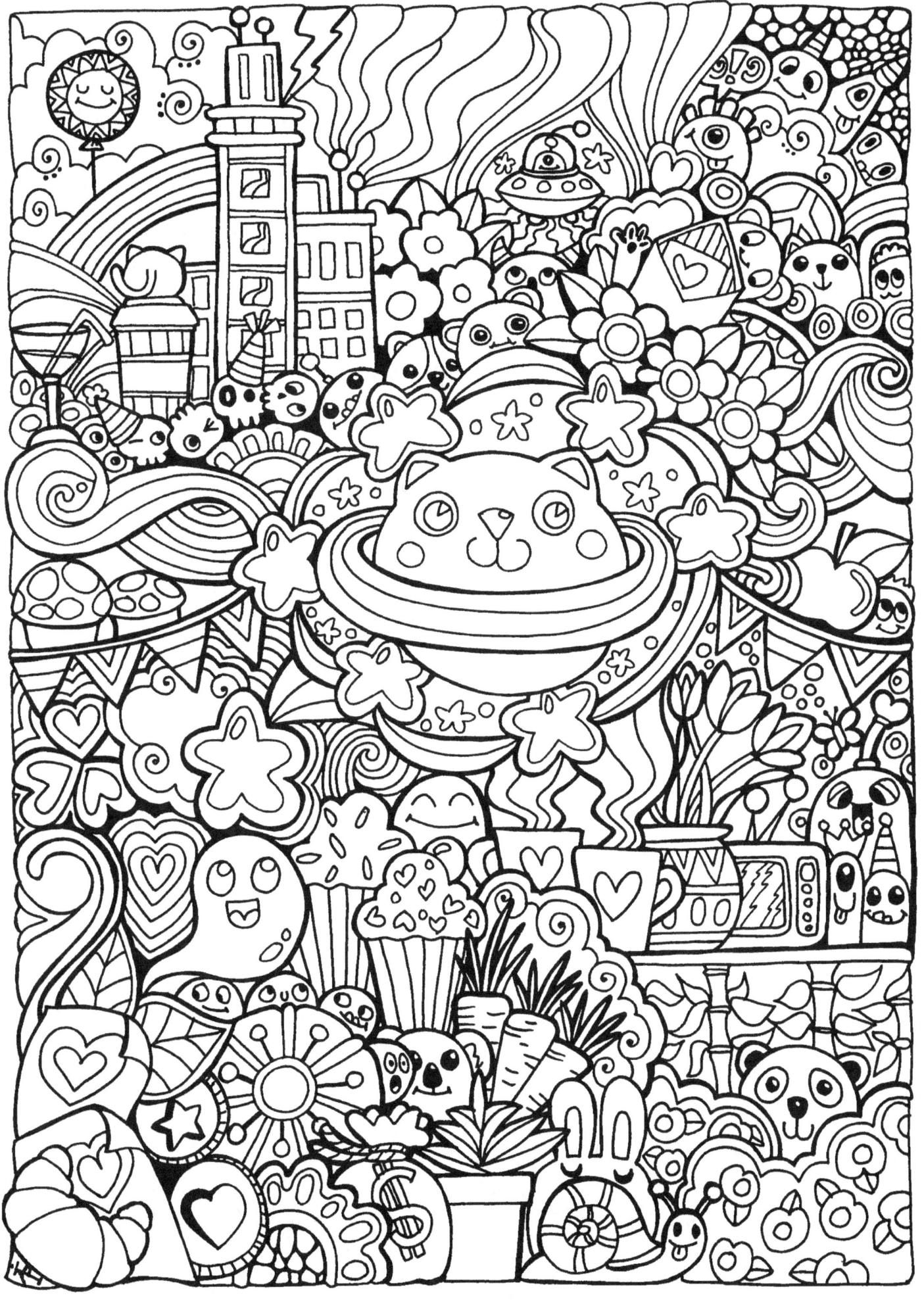

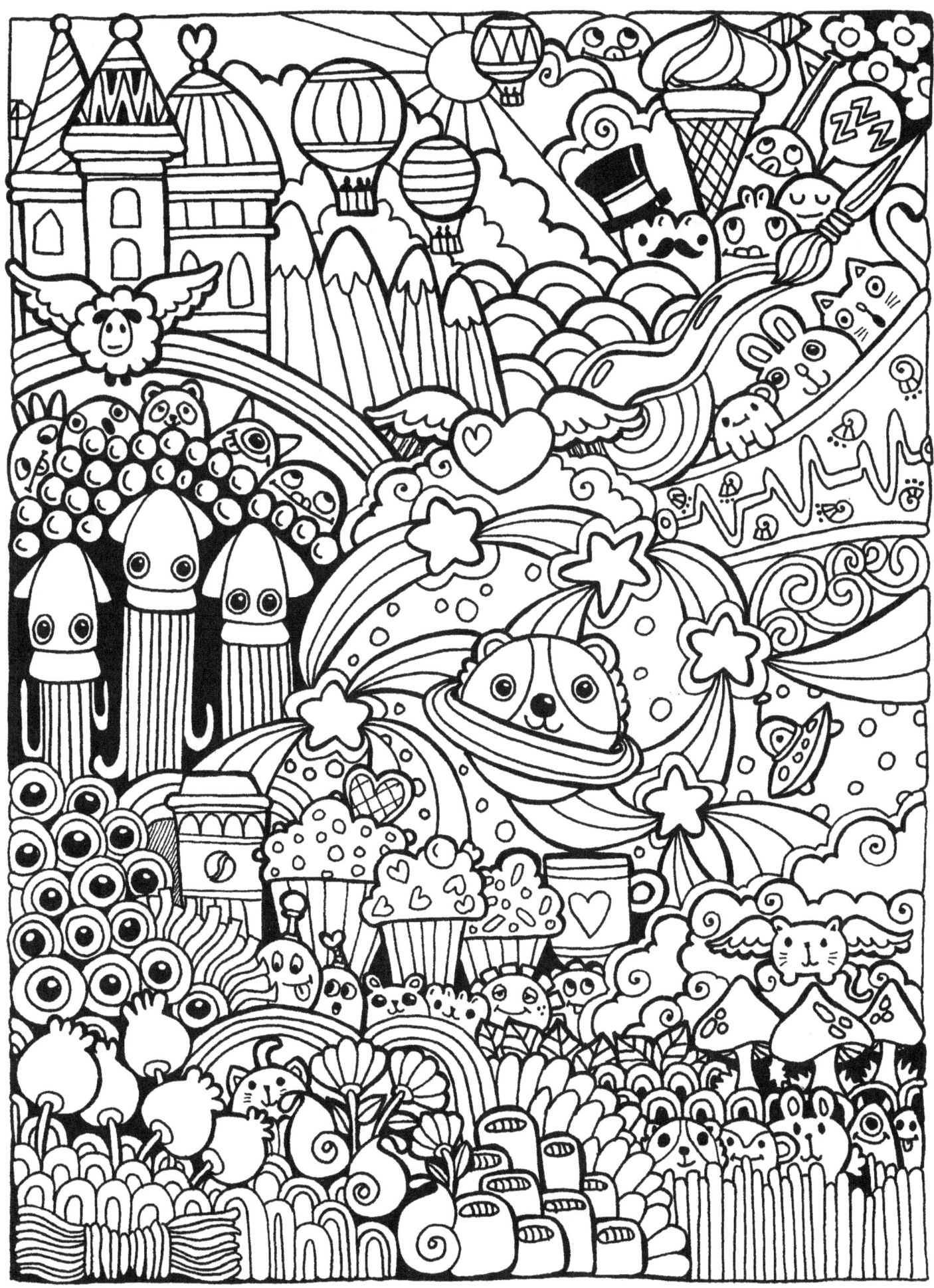

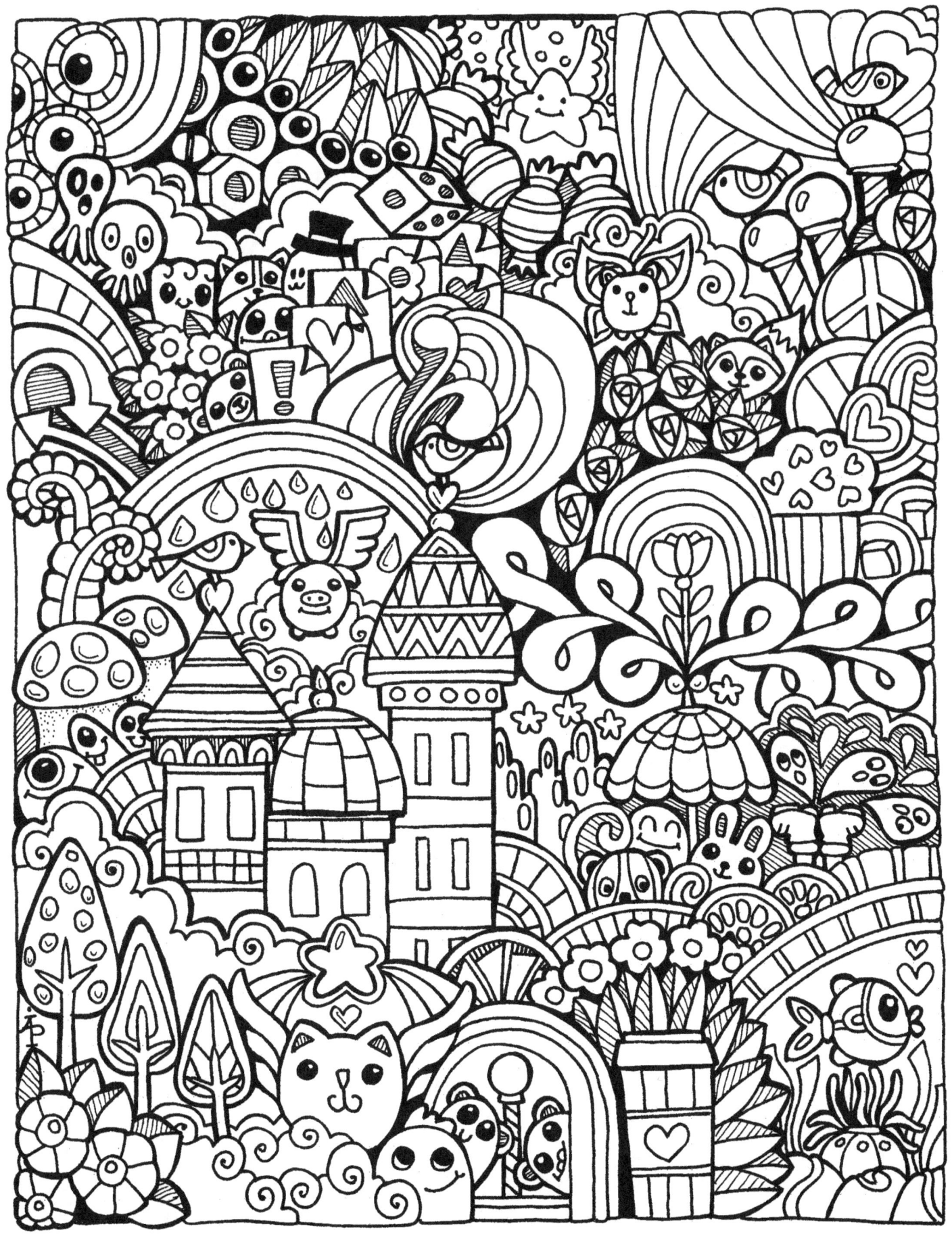

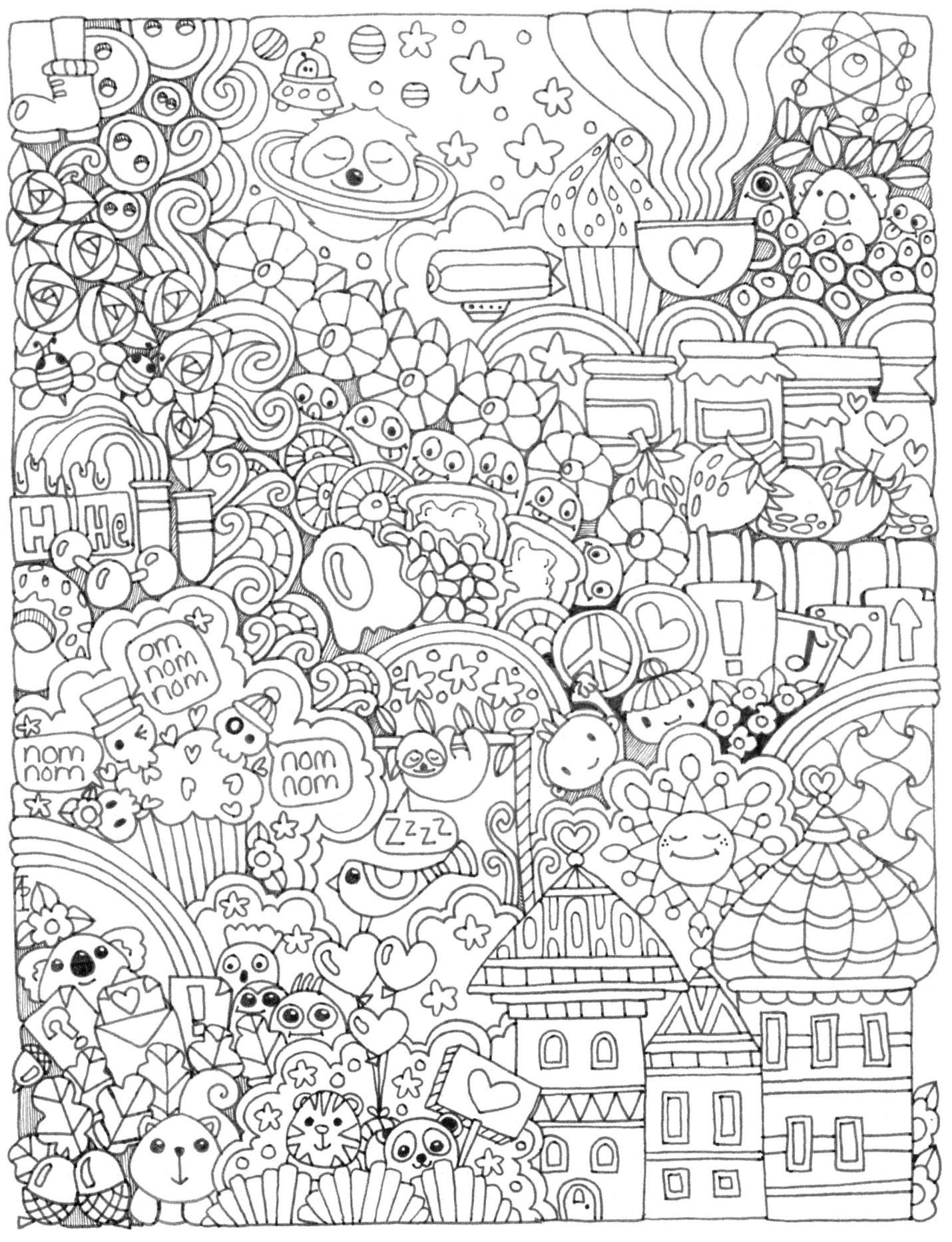

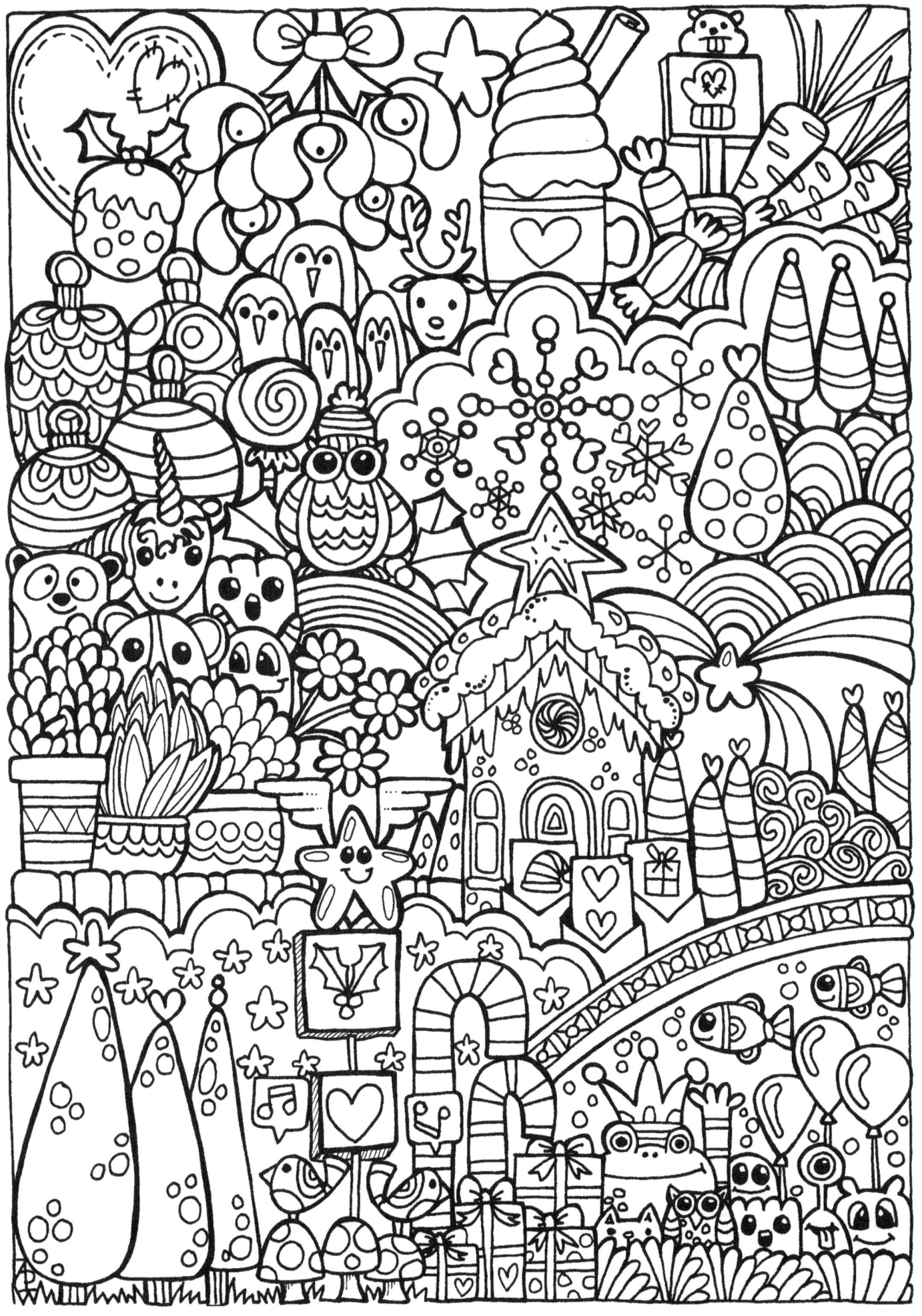

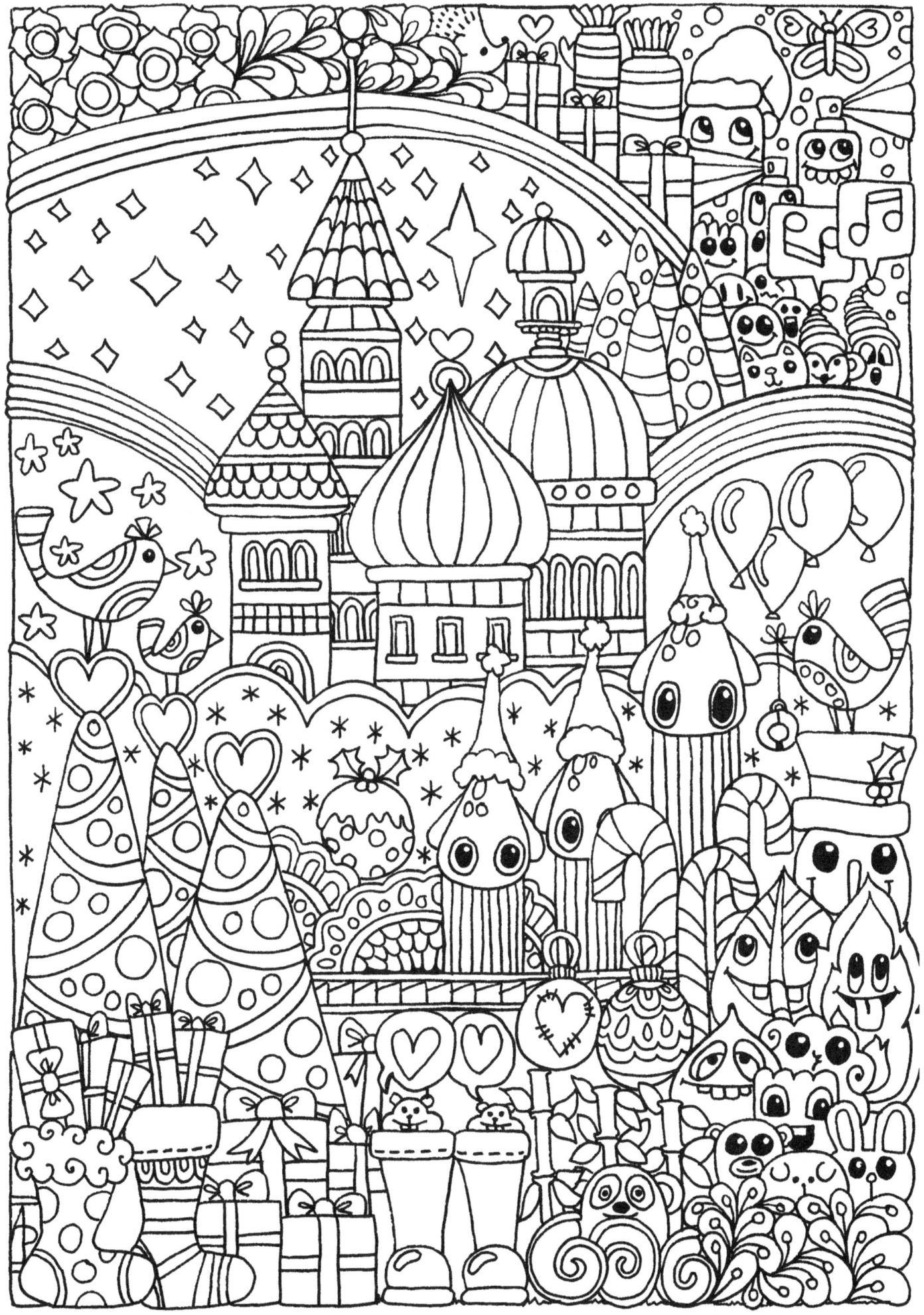

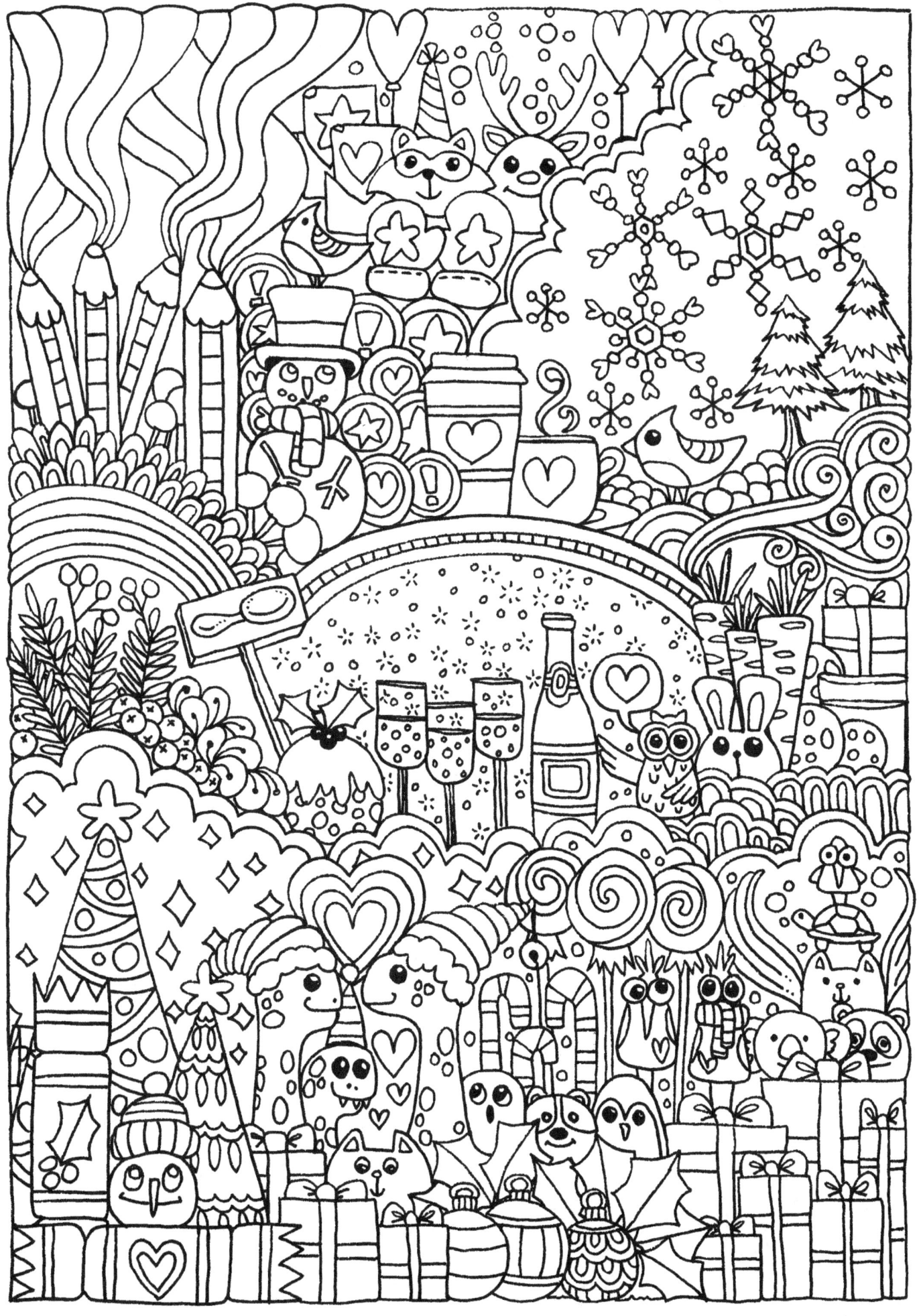

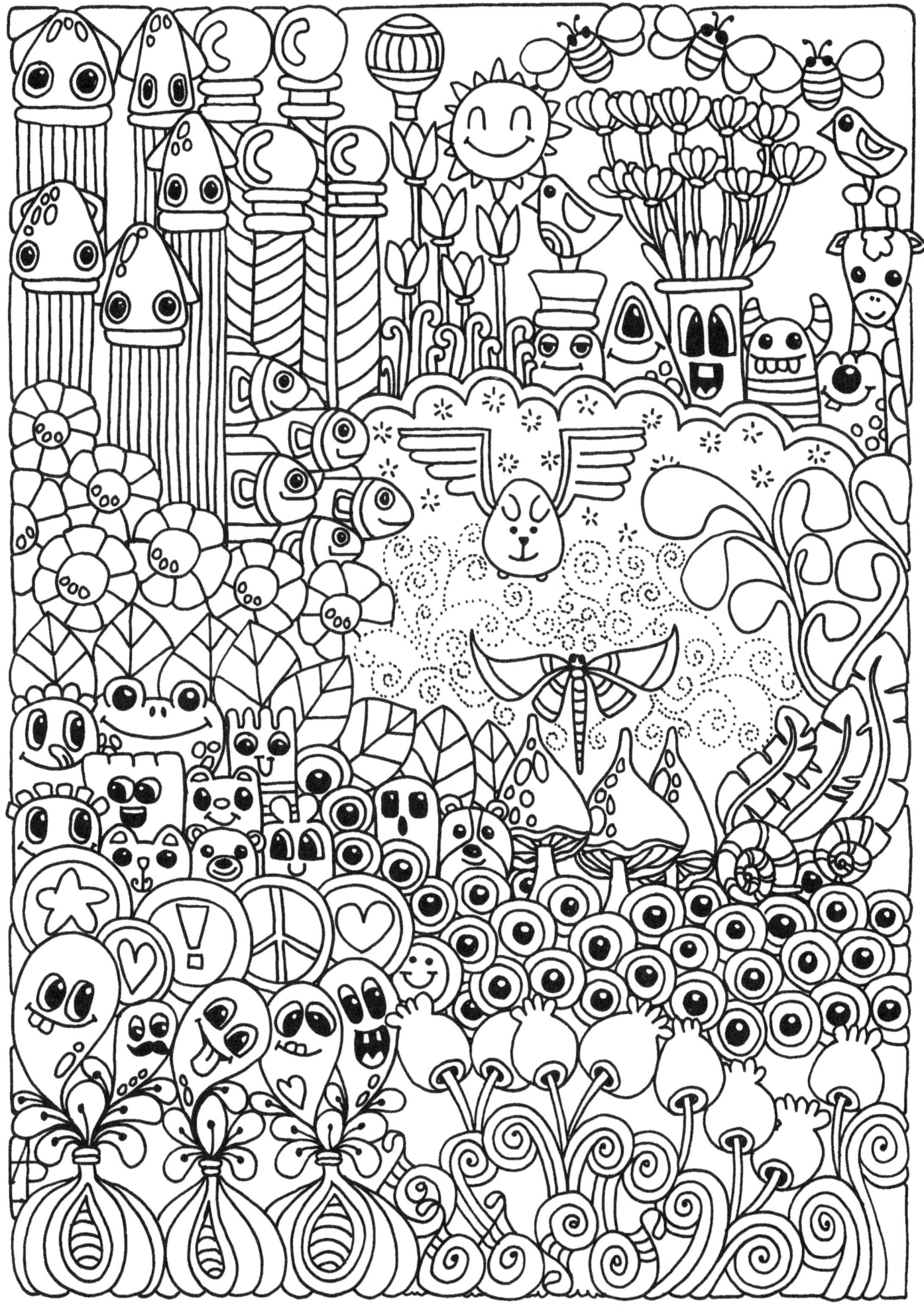

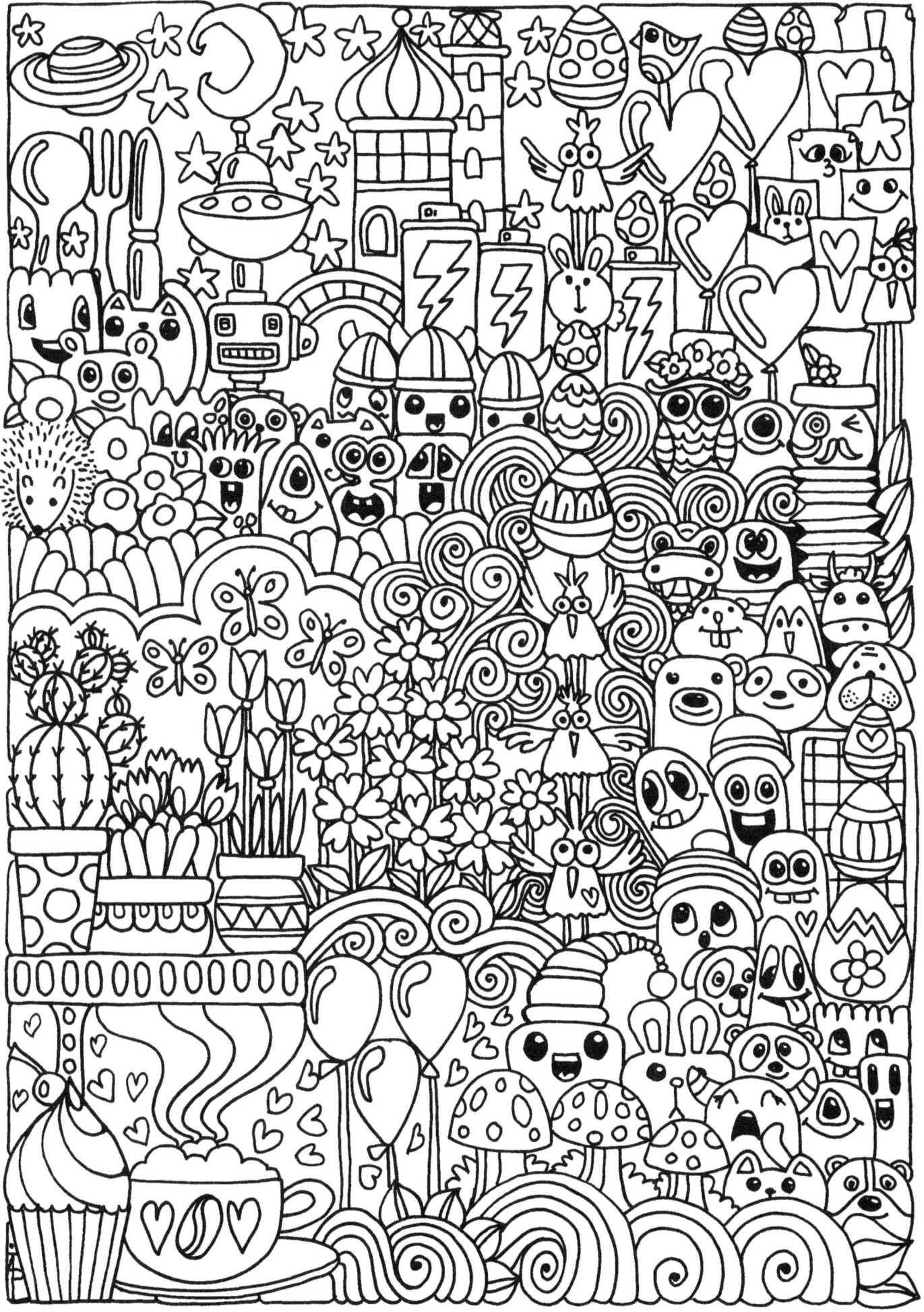

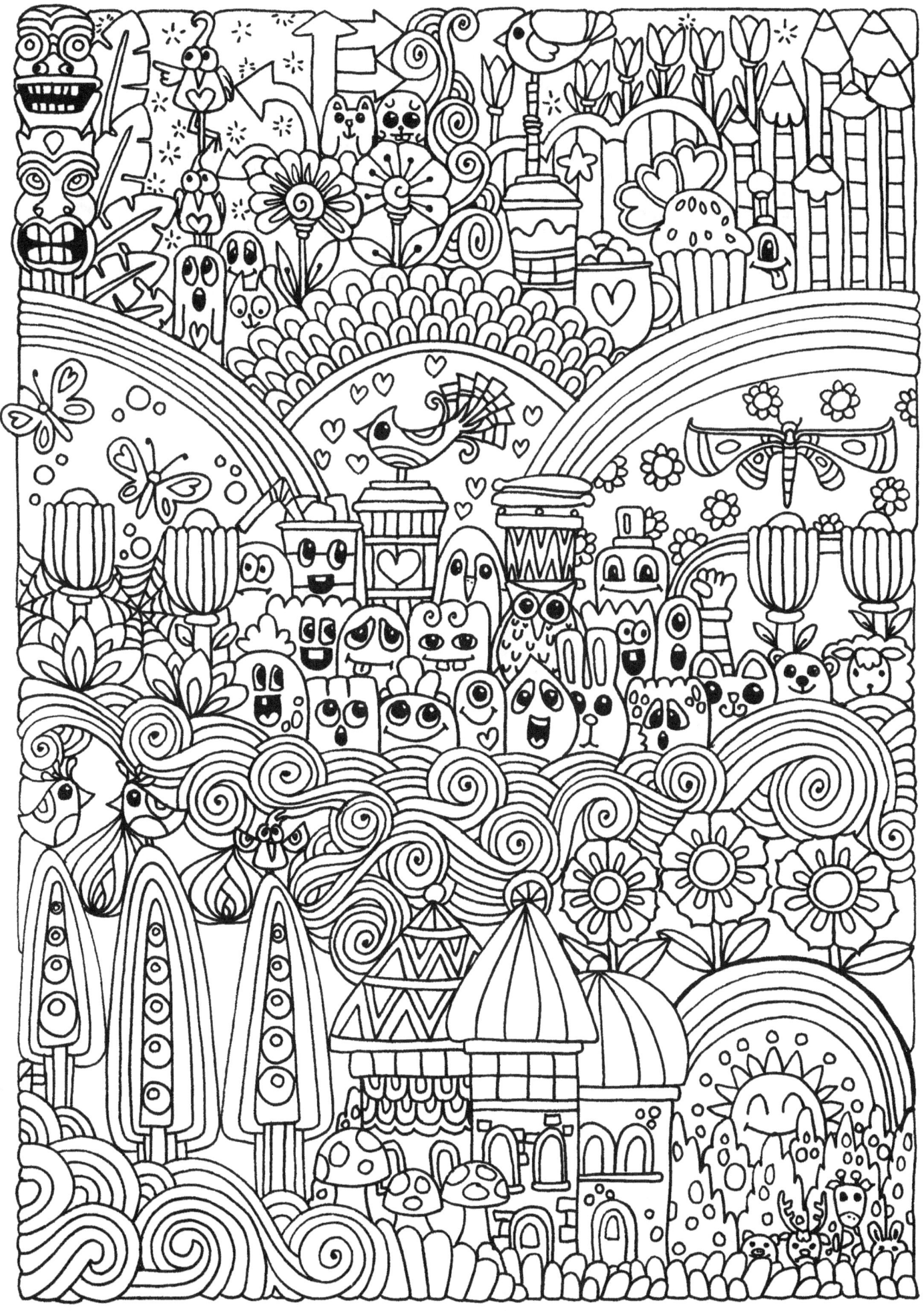

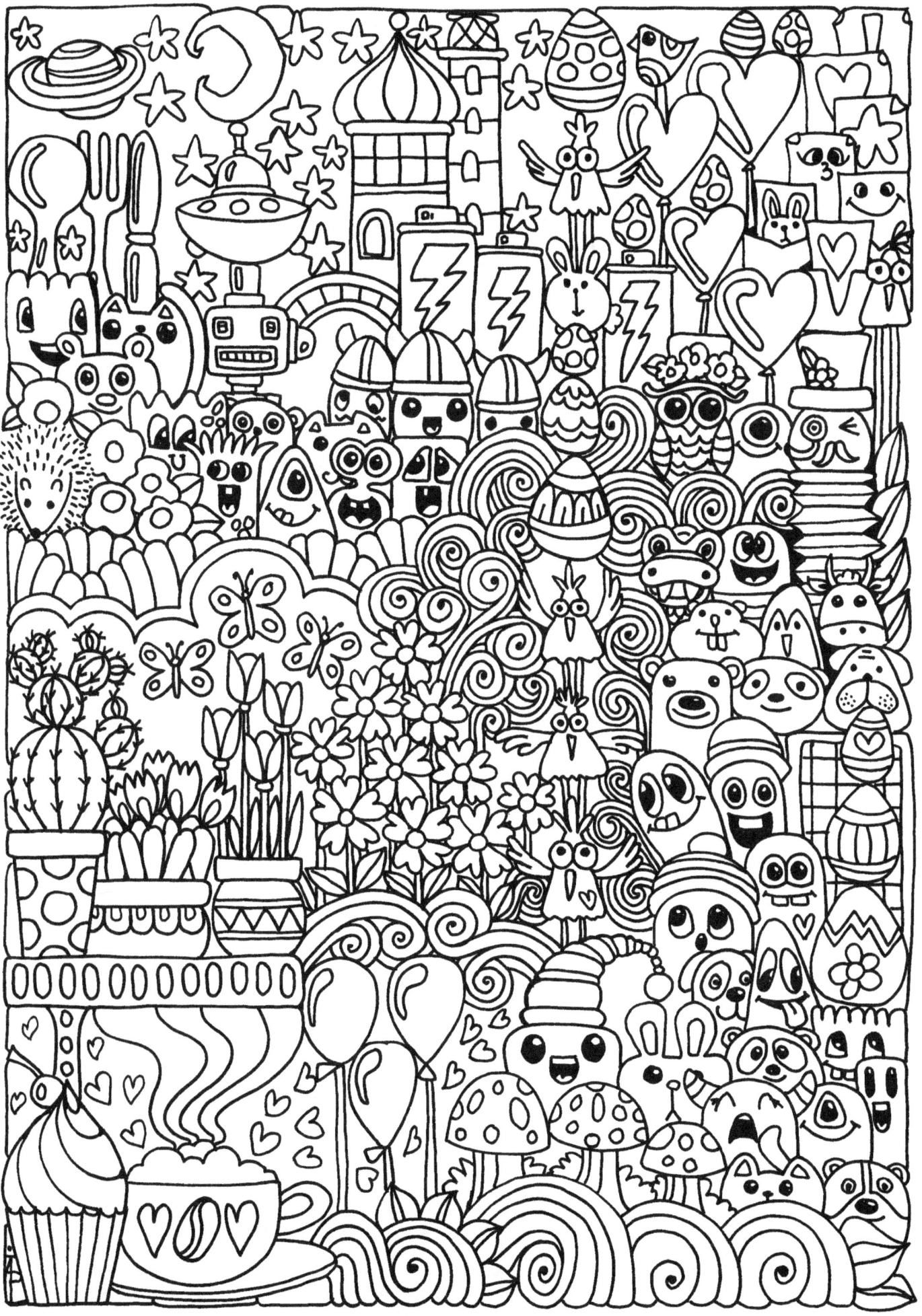

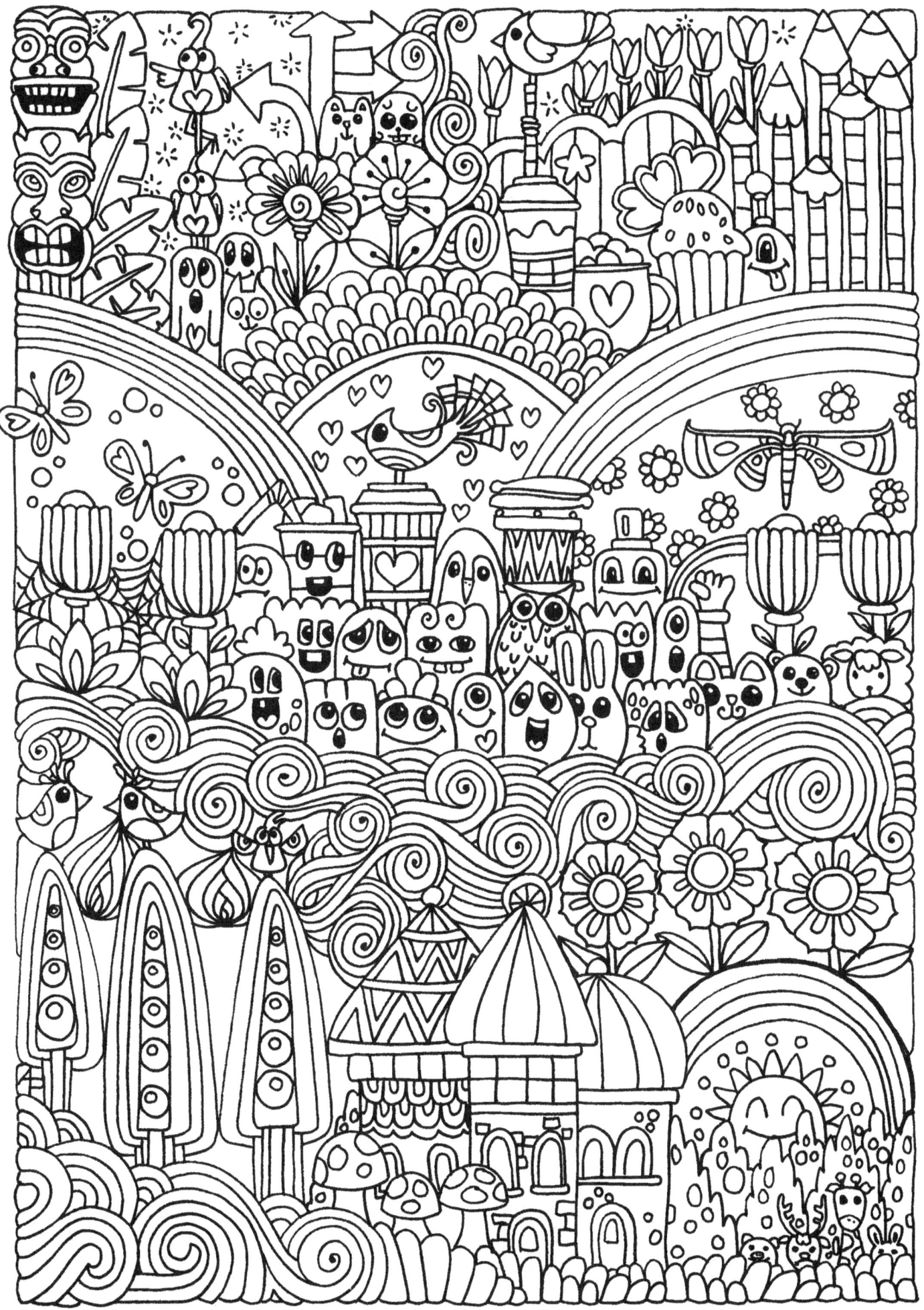

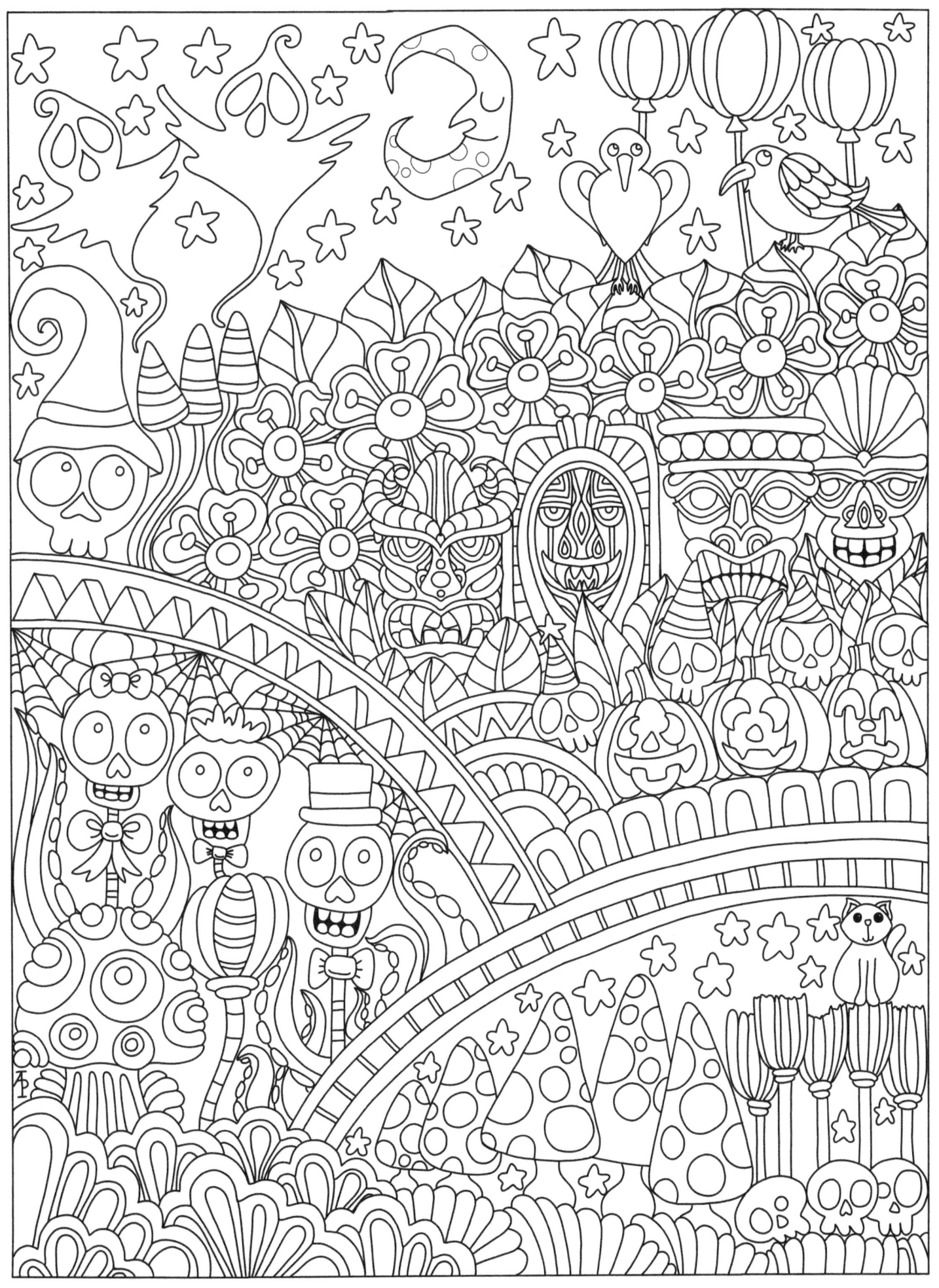

www.ingramcontent.com/pod-product-compliance
Lightning Source LLC
Chambersburg PA
CBHW081121240526
45470CB00019B/2776